Teaching Social Skills to Youth

4th Edition

Also from the Boys Town Press

Mental Health from Diagnosis to Delivery
Building Resiliency in Youth: A Trauma-Informed Guide for Working with Youth in Schools
Building Resiliency in Children: A Trauma-Informed Activity Guide for Children
Building Resiliency in Teens: A Trauma-Informed Workbook for Teens
Well-Managed Schools
Tools for Teaching Social Skills in School
More Tools for Teaching Social Skills in School
Positive Alternatives to Suspension
deCoding Respect
Everyone's Talking: Stories to Engage Middle Schoolers in Social Conversation
Take Two: Skill-Building Skits You Have Time to Do!
13 & Counting: Rescue Me?
13 & Counting: Be the Difference!
13 & Counting: Does a Hamburger Really Have to Be Round?
GRIT & Bear It!
ZEST: Live It!
Safe and Healthy Secondary Schools
Working with Aggressive Youth
No Room for Bullies
No Room for Bullies: Lesson Plans for Grades 5-8
No Room for Bullies: Lesson Plans for Grades 9-12
Common Sense Parenting®
Common Sense Parenting® of Toddlers and Preschoolers

For Adolescents

Middle School Misfits
He's Not Just Teasing
Am I Weird?
I Lost My BFF
The Good, the Bad, and the Backstory
Friend Me!
Boundaries: A Guide for Teens
A Good Friend
Basic Social Skills for Youth

Please turn to the back of this book to find a list of popular children's titles (Grades K-6) that teach vital social and life skills.

For a Boys Town Press catalog, call **1-800-282-6657**
or visit our website: **BoysTownPress.org**

Boys Town National Hotline®
1-800-448-3000
A crisis, resource, and referral number for kids and parents

Teaching Social Skills to Youth

4th Edition

An Easy-to-Follow Guide to Teaching 196 Basic to Complex Life Skills

JEFF TIERNEY, M.ED. AND ERIN GREEN, M.S.
Contributing Authors: Tom Dowd, M.A. and Kat McGrady, Ed.D., LCPC, NCC

BOYS TOWN. Press

Boys Town, Nebraska

Teaching Social Skills to Youth, 4th Edition

Published by Boys Town Press
Boys Town, NE 68010
Copyright © 2022 by Father Flanagan's Boys' Home

ISBN: 978-1-944882-97-6

Boys Town Press is the publishing division of Boys Town, a national organization serving children and families.

Publisher's Cataloging in Publication

Names: Tierney, Jeff, author. | Green, Erin, author. | Dowd, Tom (Tom P.), author. | McGrady, Kat, author.

Title: Teaching social skills to youth : an easy-to-follow guide to teaching 196 basic to complex life skills / Jeff Tierney and Erin Green ; contributing authors: Tom Dowd and Kat McGrady.

Description: 4th edition. | Boys Town, NE : Boys Town Press, [2022] | Includes index. | Audience: grades K-12.

Identifiers: ISBN: 978-1-944882-97-6

Subjects: LCSH: Social skills in children--Study and teaching. | Social interaction in children--Study and teaching. | Interpersonal relations in children--Study and teaching. | Social learning--Study and teaching. | Socialization--Study and teaching. | Emotional maturity--Study and teaching. | Executive functions (Neuropsychology) | Children--Life skills guides. | BISAC: EDUCATION / Behavioral Management. | EDUCATION / Counseling / General. | EDUCATION / Special Education / Behavioral, Emotional & Social Disabilities. | EDUCATION / Decision-Making & Problem Solving. | PSYCHOLOGY / Interpersonal Relations. | PSYCHOLOGY / Psychotherapy / Child & Adolescent. | PSYCHOLOGY / Psychopathology / Attention-Deficit Disorder (ADD-ADHD)

Classification: LCC: HQ783 .T54 2022 | DDC: 303.3/207--dc23

15 14 13 12 11 10 9 8 7 6 5 4 3 2

Acknowledgments

We thank the following Boys Town staff members for their contributions to the fourth edition of this book and for their commitment to providing a valuable resource for all those who strive to improve the lives of children: Barb Vollmer, Angie Powers, Dr. Patrick Tyler, Scott Hartman, Lisa Batenhorst, Jon Jelley, Jil Fisher, Kathy Kirby, Olivia Crimiel-Minor, Chief William Clark, Jennifer Buth-Bell, Denise Pratt, Lynette Zurek, Paula Kohrt, Doug Vanden Hoek, Stan Graeve, and Mike Sterba.

Table of Contents

CHAPTER 7

Introduction to Social Skills Teaching

*S*hay never wanted to hear the word no! And before she learned the skill of "Accepting 'No' for an Answer," most of the adults around her never wanted to get stuck telling her no. The 11-year-old had learned, from years of experience, to get what she wanted by giving a look that sent the message: "I REALLY will scream and fight right here if you say no!" Unfortunately, her parents, teachers, and others buckled under the threat.

What they didn't understand, however, was how much that was hurting Shay. Her relationships with her peers and other adults suffered. Whenever she heard no, screaming, crying, and arguing quickly followed. Her behavior continued to escalate until more trouble ensued.

Shay's education in how to appropriately accept no started in school when her teacher taught the skill as part of a classroom lesson. The teacher also sent the students home with posters that described the steps of "Accepting 'No' for an Answer":

* *Look at the person.*
* *Say, "Okay."*
* *Stay calm (avoid arguing or complaining).*
* *If you disagree, ask later.*

Shay's parents started working with her on learning the steps of the skill. After weeks of practice and the use of appropriate consequences, Shay had the steps down, and her behavior began to improve. Now when someone tells her no, she isn't always happy about it but she does a much better job accepting no than she ever has before. Shay also gets along better with her parents and teacher, and they are proud of her progress. For this child, one simple, basic skill made a huge difference in her behavior, her personality, and the way she gets along with others.

1

Social skills, such as "Accepting 'No' for an Answer," are nothing new – except to the children (and adults) who don't have them or know how to use them. The earlier children and adolescents (and even adults) learn and know how to use social skills, the more successful they can be.

Everyone needs social skills. Social skills are the tools that enable people to communicate, learn, ask questions, ask for help, get their needs met in appropriate ways, get along with others, make friends and develop healthy relationships, protect themselves, and generally be able to interact with anyone and everyone they meet in their journey through life.

While the long-term goals of social skill instruction are generalization (using the right skill at the right time in the right situation) and internalization (making skills a natural part of one's everyday life), the short-term benefits to teaching children skills cannot be overstated. In fact, when children learn foundational skills, such as "Following Instructions," "Accepting 'No' for an Answer," and "Disagreeing Appropriately," it enables whoever is teaching to continue teaching and sets the stage for instruction in more advanced and complex skills. In other words, if a child knows how to appropriately follow instructions, they can be directed to adopt and use a variety of prosocial behaviors that make up other beneficial skills. It is the repertoire of skills a child develops over time that shapes how they function in society.

According to Dr. Stephen Greenspan (2012), who has studied and written about the importance of social competence for more than 30 years, social incompetence contributes to a range of challenges–from gullibility to an inability to accept corrective feedback to violence–that undermine children (and adults). Because of the preva- lence of and risks associated with social in- competence, when discussing achievement and teacher success, Greenspan believes such social and emotional factors as class- room harmony to be even more important than achievement test scores.

A child who does not learn social skills and the basics of social interactions is at tre- mendous risk for failure in the classroom, juvenile delinquency, being ostracized by positive peers, or being adversely influ- enced by negative peers. Children who are never taught social skills develop their own habits and devices for getting their needs met, habits and devices that often conflict with what society views as acceptable be- havior. The result can be an adolescent and adult life punctuated by violence, drug and alcohol abuse, failed relationships, incar- ceration, and the frustration of never real- izing one's goals.

Boys Town's Approach to Teaching Skills

Social skill instruction and achieving skill competency are so important to the success of young people and adults that they are an integral part of every program Boys Town offers. Boys Town has been caring for children since 1917, and while times and children's problems have radi- cally changed over the years, our approach of combining the "head" – child care tech- nology, research, and innovation – and the "heart" – compassion, caring, and loving guidance – has remained constant. All kids – especially those who are at risk or in dan- ger of becoming at risk – need the kind of attention and help that brings about posi- tive, lasting changes in their way of think- ing, feeling, and behaving. Social skills hold the key to unlocking the potential for good that every child possesses.

Boys Town's mission is to change the way America cares for children and families. Accomplishing that mission on a day-to-day basis is difficult, requiring commitment, sacrifice, and skilled caregivers. In addition to our long-range goals, Boys Town first provides a safe environment for young people where they can put their lives in order and, in many cases, begin healing wounds that run very deep.

Our Continuum of Care is unique to Boys Town and provides a tightly linked spectrum of research-proven services based on the Boys Town Model®. Children and families can begin services at any point along the continuum and move to other levels, depending on their progress or needs. This unique approach enables us to help more children and families in more ways, with the same expectations for positive results. For children, this means being successful in school, at home, and on the job while growing into productive citizens. For families, it means having a safe home, being able to solve problems, and staying together. For communities, it means stronger, empowered families and citizens who contribute to the good of society.

The famed Village of Boys Town, Nebraska, remains the national headquarters for Boys Town and is the research, program development, and administrative center of the organization. Boys Town's outreach is national in scope, with sites across the country providing life-changing care. Even more children and families receive benefits through our community support services and programs.

Boys Town youth care and health care services meet each child and family exactly where they are so they get the right kind of care, at the right time, in the right way. Whether caring for a child in crisis, treating complex health care conditions, or helping families find the parenting resources they need, we deliver expert, compassionate care and have a proven track record of helping children and families heal and grow in mind, body, and spirit.

Residential Treatment Center

The Boys Town Residential Treatment Center is changing the lives of children ages 5 to 18 who have severe behavioral and mental health problems through a proven, medically directed treatment program. Our goal is to help children gain the self-assurance and academic and social skills needed to succeed in life.

The Residential Treatment Center at Boys Town National Research Hospital® is licensed by the Nebraska Department of Health and accredited by The Joint Commission. The Center is licensed by the Nebraska Department of Health and accredited by The Joint Commission.

Facility Secure – Our treatment program is specifically designed to offer medically directed care for more seriously troubled youth who require supervision, safety, and therapy but do not require inpatient psychiatric care. The program offers around-the-clock supervision, locked facilities, and numerous other safety and program features.

Intervention and Assessment Services

Boys Town Intervention and Assessment Services® provide emergency, short-term, 24-hour care in a residential setting for boys and girls ages 10 to 18. Many have been abused and/or neglected, are runaways, or have come through the juvenile justice system. When youth enter these services, professionally trained staff members begin assessing their safety, health, and service needs in order to determine and plan for the best permanent care arrangement.

The primary goals at this level of service are to remove youth from dangerous situations and/or provide temporary care. Every child receives an immediate behavioral intervention. Youth may also receive additional clinical assessments based on their needs and the desire of the referral source. Staff members also teach youth social skills, ensure that they continue to go to school, and work with youth (and when possible, their families) to develop individualized, skill-focused service plans that address behavior problem areas. Whenever possible, staff members help youth work toward reunification with their family.

Family Home Program

At this service level, youth with serious behavioral or emotional problems live in a family-style home and receive teaching and care from professionally trained married couples called Family-Teachers®. Six to eight boys or girls, usually ages 10 to 18, live in each home. The couple and a full-time Assistant Family-Teacher® are responsible for providing structured supervision for youth in their daily living and care activities. This includes meeting the educational, medical, psychological, emotional, and behavioral needs of the youth in care. A major focus of this program is teaching youth social, independent-living, and educational skills, and helping them build healthy relationships with others. With a focus on reunification, the Family-Teaching staff works with families to achieve permanency, safety, and child well-being.

Foster Family Services

Boys Town Foster Family Services® is a community-based program where professionally trained Foster Parents provide care and support to children of all ages, infancy through adolescence. Foster parents help meet the behavioral, emotional, and educational needs of the children in their care. Service intensity ranges from highly intensive to less intensive, based upon the needs of the child. With a focus on reunification, Foster Family Services utilize a strength-based, team approach to work with families to achieve safety, permanency, and well-being. Foster Parents receive 24/7 support from Boys Town professionals.

In-Home Family Services

Boys Town values families and believes that children who can be safe at home belong at home. The main goal of In-Home Family Services is to prevent children from being placed outside of the home and/or to reunify them with their family if outside placement is necessary.

One of our fastest-growing programs, Boys Town In-Home Family Services® is a family-centered, skill-based intervention for families that are in or near a crisis situation, and are at risk for having a child removed from the home. Intervention duration ranges from short term to long term, and service intensity ranges from highly intensive to less intensive, depending on a family's needs. Boys Town Family Consultants are available 24/7 and work with families in their homes to help caregivers build on their strengths, improve their parenting skills, and identify community resources and supports. Services focus on the entire family. Consultants also help families learn how to solve problems that may threaten their stability or their children's safety after the intervention ends.

Community Support Services

Boys Town Community Support Services provide resources and valuable information to parents, families, and professionals across the United States, and direct care for children and families in certain affiliate site communities. The main goal of programs at this service level is to help people help themselves by providing tools, training, resources, and other techniques based on Boys Town's research-proven approach to the care and education of children and families.

CARE COORDINATION SERVICES

Care Coordination Services provides case-management services to children and families facing significant challenges, such as involvement in the child welfare system or raising a child with behavioral or mental health issues. The family may be intact or, in some cases, one or more children may be placed outside of the home. Boys Town's trained Consultants work with families to help them identify and access the right services at the right time, build and maintain family stability, and develop quality parenting skills. Boys Town Consultants are available to families 24 hours a day, seven days a week for crisis support

OUTPATIENT BEHAVIORAL HEALTH

Outpatient Behavioral Health therapists work with children from infancy to early adulthood and their families to assess and treat youth issues. With the involvement of parents, therapists develop service plans for youth with difficult problems like Attention-Deficit/Hyperactivity Disorder (ADHD), anger management, bedtime and sleep disorders, out-of-control behaviors, learning challenges, and depression. Psychologists and therapists work with families, physicians, teachers, and others to extend care beyond the "therapy hour" to ensure long-term success.

SCHOOL-BASED PROGRAMS

Boys Town views schools as an integral part of the community and provides a variety of programs that can support or enhance the educational environment. Boys Town's education training and consultation programs teach school staff how to implement classroom management methods intended to promote a safe and effective learning environment. These programs use the Boys Town Education Model®, which focuses on skills teaching, relationship building, and effective discipline procedures. Boys Town also has other school-based programs that supplement existing curricula with instruction on issues such as connecting parents to school, character building, and adolescent reading, or provide behavioral assessments for youth and support to education staff.

BOYS TOWN SCHOOLS®

School programs operated by Boys Town help students with learning or behavioral problems so they can be successful in the classroom. This includes students who are being served by Boys Town programs or have struggled or failed in mainstream schools. Specially trained Boys Town teachers and administrators provide instruction to help meet children's unique behavioral, emotional, and educational needs. School staff members base their instruction for students on the principles of the Boys Town Education Model, which include skills teaching, relationship building, and effective discipline procedures.

BOYS TOWN NATIONAL HOTLINE®
(800.448.3000)

The **Boys Town National Hotline** is a free resource and counseling service that assists callers 24/7, 365 days a year, nationwide. Open to everyone, but with an emphasis on helping children and parents, the Hotline has trained professional counselors who provide emergency or direct assistance, or refer callers to community resources. Since opening in 1989, the Hotline has handled more than eight million calls and has helped prevent thousands of suicides nationwide.

The Hotline also provides a website created especially for teens – **www.YourLife YourVoice.org**. Teens can share information with other teens, ask questions and get answers to the challenges they are facing, and access assistance from trained counselors in emergency or crisis situations. The site enables and encourages teens to share their problems, concerns, and challenges in positive, creative ways in a safe online environment.

BOYSTOWN.ORG/PARENTING

Boystown.org/parenting is a free online resource for parents that offers tips, advice, resources, and guidance. This website contains practical, skill-based materials and information for parents and caregivers of children of all ages. All of the practical, helpful content is based on Boys Town's positive approach to parenting and research-proven caregiver strategies.

COMMON SENSE PARENTING®

Common Sense Parenting provides parents and other caregivers with proven techniques that can help them build good family relationships, prevent and correct misbehavior, use consequences to improve behavior, teach self-control, and remain calm. This instruction is generally provided in the community and schools in both formal and informal settings.

BOYS TOWN PRESS®

The **Boys Town Press** publishes books, posters, multi-media products, and other resources to assist children, parents, caregivers, educators, and professionals who work with youth and families. Publications are based on the proven youth care, parenting, and educational techniques developed and used in Boys Town programs across the country.

All of our programs and materials are rooted in the Boys Town Model.

BOYS TOWN RESEARCH

Research is critical to our mission and plays an important role in the development and delivery of our youth care and health care services to families, children, and patients. Boys Town is internationally recognized as a research leader in hearing, language and related communication disorders, and pediatric neuroscience. Through each of our research centers, we translate findings directly into the care we provide for children, families, and patients.

ADVOCATES FOR JUVENILE JUSTICE REFORM

Children should be treated as children, not adults, especially when they violate the law and enter the juvenile justice system. We believe in rehabilitation and redemption, not arbitrary, discriminatory, or punitive intervention. We advocate for a fair and just system that takes into consideration a child's age, psychosocial development, and cognitive abilities. Given the right interventions and support, no child is beyond hope.

The Boys Town Model

To understand the concept of helping children learn new skills and behaviors so they can competently use them in society, one must first realize that we are in the "business" of bringing healing and hope to children and families. Everything we do is rooted in the human experience – the successes, the failures, the progress, the obstacles. Children are human beings, not products on an assembly line. Boys Town's caregivers are not robots programmed to perform the same task, the same way, every day. It is true that technology and theory (the head) are necessary, but so is genuine compassion and concern (the heart) and treating each youth as an individual with unique problems. Technology without compassion is pure manipulation; love and compassion without good science is pure sentimentality.

While the Boys Town Model has its basis in learning theory, it has not adopted a "mechanistic" view of how a child learns, as have other models that take this approach. In the Boys Town Model, the child is an active participant in the teaching and learning that occurs. The child isn't merely told how to behave; they learn positive behaviors and how to choose to use them in many different situations. This "empowerment," or self-help, approach combines the active participation of the child with the active teaching of the parent, caretaker, or teachers. The strength of this approach is that it teaches children prosocial skills and helps them build healthy relationships with others.

The goal of this approach is not to control children, but to help them take control of their own lives. This is an ongoing learning process. Boys Town's teaching methods utilize behavioral principles, while allowing children to integrate their thoughts and feelings into this learning process. And, unlike many other learning theory models, Boys Town effectively uses external reinforcement, where appropriate, to promote and maintain skill-learning and relationship development. This allows children to change intrinsically. Inadequate thought patterns change, negative feelings diminish, and inappropriate behaviors are replaced by positive behaviors for the youth and others.

In addition to teaching skills, other hallmarks of the Boys Town Model include:

- Safety, permanency, and well-being
- Family engagement
- People closest to children and families are the primary change agents
- Behavioral orientation
- Individualized skill acquisition
- Replicable, outcome-driven programs
- Internal and external collaboration

Together, these hallmarks comprise a proven, research-based, outcomes-oriented, and effective approach to helping children and families. In our programs, we expect kids to get better, and they do.

While all of the elements of our Model share equal importance, teaching skills is what helps kids learn new ways of thinking, new ways of feeling good, and new ways of behaving. Through teaching, we give kids the skills they need to take control of their lives and be successful. Whether it's a parent who wants to teach his daughter the skill of problem-solving, a staff member in a youth shelter trying to help a boy learn anger control strategies, or a teacher looking to equip a student with the skill of staying on task or following instructions, teach-

7

ing skills is the key to healthy child development and replacing problem behaviors with positive alternative behaviors.

ADDRESSING Sociocultural Influences

ADDRESSING is an acronym that stands for **A**ge and generational influences, **De**velopmental and acquired **D**isabilities, **Re**ligion and spiritual orientation, **E**thnicity, **S**ocioeconomic status, **S**exual orientation, **I**ndigenous heritage, **N**ational origin, and **G**ender.

The ADDRESSING Model is a tool caregivers can use to help formulate culturally responsive treatment methods that better serve children and families by recognizing and respecting their individual identities. The model encourages caregivers to broaden their interpretation of cultural identity beyond ethnicity and race to see and understand the significant role cultural groups, traditions, and influences play in a youth's development.

ADDRESSING, as the acronym implies, is designed to prevent caregivers from making inaccurate or sweeping generalizations based on surface-level characteristics and internalized beliefs. Using this framework or approach can broaden the caregivers' perspective by calling attention to how an individual's multicultural background influences knowledge, skills, and attitudes about their external and internal worlds. It's a model for understanding the way cultural influences affect one's worldview in addition to recognizing the various cultural influences that help shape and explain a person's identity. Caregivers who lack cultural awareness, knowledge, and skills may view certain populations or people through a flawed, distorted, or unfair lens. There-

fore, it is essential that caregivers develop their cultural responsiveness by continually learning about other cultures and beliefs, identifying biases, and assessing their own cultural perspectives (Hays, 2008).

Culturally Responsive Social Skill Instruction

When social skill instruction is part of an individualized treatment plan, cultural and ethnic factors will influence what skills are targeted, how those skills are taught, and what skill components are included. For example, many cultures consider it a sign of disrespect for a youth to make direct eye contact with an adult. However, almost all of the social skills taught in the Boys Town Model include the component, "Look at the person." Therefore, when teaching this specific behavior to a youth who may have been taught to avoid eye contact, a caregiver may need to modify or target the behavior for extra teaching and shape it over a longer period of time. The caregiver also should teach discrimination skills to the youth, helping them to understand that it is acceptable to look at their classroom teacher or a boss at work, but it may not be appropriate to make eye contact with elders who are from or share their culture. Other behavioral areas that may require modified goals because of culture-specific factors or influences (family, home life, economic class, ethnicity, etc.) include the following:

- Body and facial gestures
- Social coolness versus warmth
- Following directions (as opposed to seeing it as a request or an option)
- Tone and volume
- Personal space
- Displays of emotion

8

- Patterns of communication in various situations
- Manners
- Courtesy
- Roles (student, teacher, male, female, age, etc.)
- Sense of fairness and justice

Support and understanding are key when teaching children skills that may step outside their comfort level or defy the cultural expectations taught within their households. Caregivers should appreciate how a youth's culture has influenced their beliefs, behaviors, and values. Moreover, caregivers should demonstrate respect for the youth's culture and avoid undermining norms instilled at home while simultaneously supporting the development of these new skills. This can be done in a variety of ways, including...

- Acknowledging the importance of their current social norm within specific contexts.
- Discussing the value of their social or cultural norm in specific contexts.
- Brainstorming together situations/settings where the new skill would be valuable and more fitting.
- Using observational data to demonstrate or model to them the value of this new skill within certain contexts.
- Getting the family involved by asking for their support and knowledge to help the youth understand when the new skill is appropriate and when the cultural norm is appropriate. Gaining their insight and working with them can ensure the youth learns the new skill while staying true to their cultural norms.

As stated earlier, caregivers should be comfortable with understanding their own cultural identities, values, and biases so they can be more proactive and effective with the youth they serve. Additionally, caregivers should be willing to practice ongoing and consistent critical self-reflection in order to ensure that cultural differences do not lead to care and treatment goals that do not align with the youth's needs. Caregivers should begin by recognizing their own identities within the ADDRESSING framework and how those identities shape their viewpoints and interactions. Once this understanding of self is in place, it may be easier to ask reflective questions when addressing youth needs, such as:

- Do I have any preconceived notions about this youth?
- Do my expectations align with the youth's previous experiences, background, and household norms, or do I need to readjust to meet the youth where they currently are?
- Am I educated enough about the youth's cultural background (household culture and communal culture)? Where or from whom can I gather more information to make informed decisions about the youth's social skills goals?

When teaching new social skills, it is essential that caregivers evaluate how learning a new set of skills will affect youth self-identity, both inside and outside the treatment setting. Those who feel accepted and develop a sense of belonging may begin to culturally identify and connect deeply with caregivers and other youth within the treatment setting. This deep sense of connection and belonging can foster a stronger confidence and security in self, thus leading to more healthy risk-taking behaviors (participation, engagement, friendship-seeking, etc.). Conversely, those who feel they are being forced to acculturate into the traditional American mainstream or feel less accepted by their peers may resist treatment or possibly adopt counterproductive behaviors as a response (meltdowns or tantrums, disengagement, shutting down, emotional reactivity, etc.). Careful and consistent evaluation, frequent check-ins with the youth, and adapting goals accordingly will result in more positive outcomes.

Finally, culturally competent caregivers should be aware that culture, race, and ethnicity are not to be used interchangeably as each has a distinct meaning. Culture has shared elements, including language, history, and geographic location, but there is no biological link. It can be broadly defined as the learned characteristics and way of life of a group of people, including social norms, traditions, and values. Many individuals identify as multicultural, as they belong to a variety of cultural groups. These groups could include heritage, social groups, and ethnic groups, to name a few.

Race is based on geography and physical characteristics, such as skin color or facial features, that tend to be genetically related. Race often is an aspect of an individual's self-identification, but it offers little information about the person. For example, race may identify one's social heritage but it clarifies little in terms of an individual's educational level, cultural context, or current environment. When formulating a treatment plan, knowledge of a child's race can help caregivers determine whether that youth considers themself to be part of the dominant or minority culture and the impact that will have on treatment goals.

Ethnicity tends to tie into nationality. It includes heritage, ancestry, history, and culture (norms, beliefs, dialect, cuisine, arts, etc.). Ethnicity also formulates many labels and perceptions that are not necessarily true for all members who may belong to the same ethnic group (Hays, 2008). Therefore, it is vital that treatment providers actively reflect on their own cultural biases, stereotypes, or underlying assumptions, and actively seek information to understand the youth as a whole person before determining plans for treatment.

It is also important to note that many youth identify within multiple races, ethnic affiliations, and/or cultures. In addition, unique household norms and recent cultural and societal shifts mean race, ethnicity, and cultural identification should serve as a "penciled in" blueprint rather than a "permanent marker" final product. Caregivers must avoid adopting fixed ideas of cultures, races, and ethnicities. Instead, they must be comfortable asking questions, researching, and gaining an understanding of the individual.

Including All Children's Unique Needs

Boys Town has always promoted individualized, appropriate, relevant, and sensitive treatment for all children, regardless of race, gender, faith, religion, or physical, mental, and intellectual ability. Each child has an individualized treatment plan with social skills that are tailored to fit their unique background and specific needs.

In this updated edition of *Teaching Social Skills to Youth,* several new social skills expand the boundaries of inclusion, ensuring the needs of all children are adequately met. Only in this way can fair and effective care be achieved. To be inclusive and meet the unique needs of all children, caregivers should add these two important questions to their care, treatment, and social skills planning activities:

- Considering the child's culture, gender, faith or religion, and ability, are there any special teaching strategies or social skills I need to explore and utilize?

- Am I teaching sufficient skill variations that will lead to success in the child's own culture, environment, and society at large?

As explained previously, many of the social skills include the step "Look at the person." Children of varying intellectual, developmental, or physical abilities may or may not be capable of fulfilling this step (or others). These skills are adaptable, and caregivers are encouraged to modify the skill steps to support the individual needs and abilities of a specific youth.

For example, if eye contact is challenging for a neurodivergent child, it may not be important that the child looks directly at you. Instead, some type of acknowledgment that they are listening is what you are targeting. In this case, praising approximations of the behavior is a positive way to support the child's social skill development. "Shea, nice job lifting your head when I was speaking to you!" If a child is unable to see, instead of encouraging them to "Look at the person," you might teach them to turn their body to "Face the direction of the person's voice."

Knowledge of different cultures, genders, faiths, religions, and physical, mental, and intellectual abilities is essential for effective care and treatment. Caregivers need to become aware of the experiences, values, and lifestyles inherent to all these critical areas unique to each child. Only in this way can we expect to have a positive impact on the care and development of all children.

What This Manual Offers

This manual reflects and focuses on the importance of teaching social skills to youth of all ages, the elements of social behavior (task and behavior analysis), individual and group teaching techniques, generalization of skills, the role of skill-based interventions for difficult youth problems, and the Boys Town Social Skills Curriculum itself.

Our Social Skills Curriculum features 196 skills or behaviors that are positive alternatives to many of the maladaptive and self-defeating behavior patterns in which a young person might engage. It is intended to serve as an effective resource and tool for anyone who works with children and adolescents. This includes teachers, staff members in long-term residential youth programs and youth shelters, foster parents, counselors, therapists, and others.

All 196 skills and their steps are presented in Chapter 7. In addition to being task-analyzed into their specific behaviors, the skills are also paired with specific skill types that intersect with multiple executive functions – social, emotional management, academic, ethical/moral, and independent living – and are categorized according to behaviors and situations in which they can be used to address problems or enhance a child's abilities. (See Appendices A, B, C, and D.) Use the provided code to download these appendices and the entire Social Skills Curriculum. Individual skills and their steps can be downloaded and printed.

NOTE: For ease of reading, we use the term "social skills" throughout this book when referring to all of the Curriculum skills in general. The specific skill types support ongoing development of the five competencies of social and emotional learning

– self-awareness, self-management, social awareness, relationship skills, and responsible decision-making. Social and emotional learning and its competencies will be defined and outlined beginning on page 13.

In addition to social and emotional competence, the skills overlap multiple processes of executive function and are used to better define the link between individual skills and behavior areas. Definitions of the five skill types as well as executive function begin on page 14.

Skills open the door to success for youth, no matter the setting in which they are taught. We hope these tools can contribute to and enhance your work as you bring about lasting change, instill hope, and prepare young people for the future that awaits them.

Skill Types and Social and Emotional Learning

According to Goleman (2005), there are more ways to measure success and intelligence than simply using traditional academic testing. Goleman's work outlined a multi-faceted approach to measuring competence in critical domains of life and in measuring success in school beyond academics.

Experts in "whole child" education and child development have advocated that more attention and focus be given to the social and emotional competencies of children. In the classroom, for example, educators face more difficult and challenging behaviors. Many of these challenges could be resolved (or at least minimized) if the social and emotional competence of students was adequately addressed.

The Collaborative for Academic, Social, and Emotional Learning (CASEL) defines social and emotional learning (SEL) as the process "through which children and adults understand and manage emotions, set and achieve positive goals, feel and show empathy for others, establish and maintain positive relationships, and make responsible decisions" (CASEL, 2014, p. 5).

SEL is fundamental to character development, and it is important to children's "health, ethical development, citizenship, academic learning, and motivation to achieve" (Elias et al., 2008, p. 253). In fact, research is expanding beyond this to measure the positive effects of the systematic implementation of social and emotional development strategies.

Evidence suggests that disruptive student behaviors negatively affect the academic learning of all members of a class. Not only is academic learning affected, but the lack of social and emotional competence by youth in schools contributes to harmful and risky behaviors, hopelessness, and a lack of safety.

For example, biennially, the Centers for Disease Control and Prevention (CDC) conducts a Youth Risk Behavior Survey among high school students, studying four primary areas: sexual behavior, high-risk substance abuse, experiencing violence, and mental health and suicide. This data is trended across 10 years. Recent survey data revealed the following (CDC, 2019):

- Nationally, 8.7 percent of students in grades 9 through 12 were truant or did not attend school on one or more of the 30 days prior to the survey because they felt unsafe at school, on their way to school, or on their way home from school.

- Nationally, 19.5 percent of high school students reported being bullied on school property during the 12 months

12

prior to the survey, and 15.7 percent of students reported being electronically bullied (texts, Instagram, Facebook, or other social media platforms) during the past year.

- Persistent feelings of sadness or hopelessness affected 36.6 percent of high school students. Those students reported having had those feelings almost every day for two weeks or more in a row for the past 12 months – so much so that these students stopped doing some usual activities.

- Alarmingly, 15.7 percent reported not only suicide ideation but actually having made a plan to attempt suicide during this period.

All of these numbers are trending upward, which is cause for great concern. This data supports the need for ongoing development of children's social and emotional competence.

Further, a series of meta-analyses cited by CASEL demonstrate that social-emotional learning leads to beneficial outcomes related to: social and emotional skills; attitudes about self, school, and civic engagement; social behaviors; conduct or behavioral disorders; emotional distress; and academic performance. What's more, these beneficial outcomes spanned multiple cultures, age groups, and ethnicities. The studies cited also demonstrated that early social and emotional skills development had positive, lasting effects on children and families, citing reduced costs required for public assistance, public housing, police involvement, and detention (CASEL, 2022).

The following pages describe the five competencies for social and emotional learning as defined by CASEL (2014, 2020).

Five Competencies for Social and Emotional Learning

Self-Awareness: *The ability to...*

- Recognize and label your emotions.
- Identify what triggers those emotions.
- Analyze emotions and how they affect others.
- Accurately recognize your strengths and limitations.
- Identify your own needs and values.
- Possess self-efficacy and self-esteem.

Youth who are more self-aware tend to exhibit self-confidence and a hopeful sense of the future.

Self-Management: *The ability to...*

- Set plans and work toward goals.
- Overcome obstacles.
- Manage stress.
- Seek help.
- Regulate impulses and emotions.
- Maintain attention.
- Exhibit motivation and hope.
- Persevere.

The ability to manage oneself and regulate impulses leads to fewer risky behaviors and greater achievement of goals.

Social Awareness: *The ability to...*

- Identify social cues (a particular challenge for students with Autism Spectrum Disorder).

- Predict others' feelings and reactions.
- Evaluate others' reactions.
- Show respect for others.
- Understand other points of view or perspectives.
- Appreciate diversity.
- Identify and use resources in one's family, school, and community.

The ability to exhibit empathy and identify and rely on available resources in the environment (family, school, and community) increases the likelihood that a child will develop positive relationships.

Relationship Skills: *The ability to...*
- Make friends.
- Learn cooperatively and work toward group goals.
- Communicate with others.
- Provide help to those who need it.
- Manage and express emotions in relationships while respecting diverse viewpoints.
- Resist inappropriate social pressures.

The risky behaviors identified in the Youth Risk Behavior Survey are less likely to occur when youth develop strong relationship skills.

Responsible Decision-Making: *The ability to...*
- Reflect on how current choices affect the future.
- Make decisions based on moral, personal, and ethical standards.
- Identify problems when making decisions and generate alternative options.
- Negotiate fairly.

- Become self-reflective and self-evaluative.

Ultimately, it is the goal of most parents, educators, and youth-serving professionals to ensure that the children in their care are able to develop positive, responsible decision-making skills.

Developing competencies in each of these social and emotional domains allows an individual a better opportunity to attain lifelong success in a variety of areas.

(In Appendix A, each of the five domains for social and emotional learning are paired with social skills that can be used to teach and reinforce the specific competency.)

Skill Types and Executive Function

In addition to the importance of developing social and emotional competence, recent research on the development of the whole child has identified a set of essential life skills. These skills, which center on a child's ability to plan, organize, and manage complex tasks, impact a child's ability to achieve in school, to prepare and be ready for the future workforce, and to avoid a host of other problems. While children aren't born with these skills, they are born with the capacity to develop these skills. These skills develop throughout childhood, into their teen years, and even early adulthood. The quality of their interactions with adults, peers, and the community greatly influences whether these skills are developed fully, or are diminished (Center on the Developing Child at Harvard University, 2011).

The cognitive processes referred to here are commonly known as "executive function." Incorporation of the term "executive" in referencing these skills is attributed to Karl Pribram (1973, 1976). A deficit in these skills is labeled as executive dysfunction or executive function deficit. These deficits are considered to have neurocognitive as well as behavioral symptoms (Baddeley, 1986; Wilson, Evans, Alderman, Burgess, & Emslie, 1997; Barkley, 2012). Examples of executive functions include impulse control, emotional control, flexibility, working memory, self-monitoring, planning and prioritizing, task initiation, and organization (Morin, 2014).

Here are the categories and descriptions of skill types that cross multiple executive function processes.

Social Skills

Skills in this category are related to most situations in which a person interacts with another person or other people. These situations might range from having a private, one-on-one conversation with a friend, to asking directions from a stranger, to being with a small group of people in a doctor's waiting room, to being part of a large crowd at a party. Social skills enable a person to appropriately communicate with, respond to, make a request from, and get along with other people.

Emotional Management Skills

Emotional management skills enable a person to find and maintain a balance between not feeling anything and letting one's feelings control their behavior. These skills also help a person maintain self-control, stay calm in exciting, stressful, or frustrating situations, and make good choices under pressure. One major area where this is important is anger control. People who know which skills to use to prevent or control their anger and not become physically or verbally aggressive are able to stay out of trouble and solve problems or overcome obstacles in appropriate ways.

Academic Skills

Completing homework and turning it in on time, studying, taking tests, reading, doing learning activities, and taking notes during lectures are just a few of the areas where having good academic skills are necessary. And while we usually associate academics only with school, these skills are useful in any learning situation, whether it is with a teacher in a classroom or reading a book or working on a computer to expand one's knowledge.

Ethical/Moral Skills

Skills that help a person learn positive ethics and morals contribute to building character and developing a conscience. A person's ability to use ethical/moral skills provides the "moral compass" that helps them know right from wrong, good from bad, and prosocial from antisocial. Good character stems from knowing the right thing to do and following through.

Independent-Living Skills

People are able to perform the activities of life – cooking, shopping, keeping up an apartment or house, managing finances, balancing a checkbook, looking for a job, buying a car and making payments, and many others – because they have learned how to take care of themselves. Independent-living skills prepare people to be on their own and to contribute to society as a wage earner, a good neighbor, a productive citizen, and an independent person.

For decades, Boys Town has emphasized the development of the whole child, including building social competence, so children are empowered to be lifelong self-managers and problem-solvers. Teaching social skills is an effective way of fostering children's social competence.

(In Appendix B, specific Curriculum skills are grouped according to these five skill types.)

CHAPTER 1

An Overview of Social Skills Training

Teaching social skills to youth is a daunting task that requires perseverance and dedication. It is a process that also calls for constant repetition and practice if caregivers are to make a critical impact on children's future development and overall social competence. Social competence, individual social behavior, and their outcomes require that youth learn social skills that can develop and improve their ability to communicate effectively, solve problems, maintain self-control, and enjoy self-efficacy.

This is a tall order because what has been taught and modeled for some youth is often inadequate and sometimes dysfunctional, creating serious development and life-event problems. This is especially true for youth who have contact with social services, the juvenile justice system, mental health services, and youth intervention programs.

Social Skills Training and Social Competence

Social competence is the outcome of different behavioral, cognitive, and emotional components. Competence suggests that one has the ability to perform a given task or set of tasks in a way that is deemed acceptable by others. When looking at social

skills and competence, we are interested in how a person is validated by their current social circle or environment. What makes social skills training challenging is understanding how the environment changes, and how the social validity of every social skill is dependent on the ability of youth to make necessary adjustments to the people and situations within that environment.

Defining the concept of social skills has been challenging ever since its inception. Depending on how a skill is viewed, most definitions focus on individual behavior and its effects and outcomes upon others. Gresham, Van, and Cook (2006) define social skills as representing "a set of competencies that (1) facilitate initiating and maintaining positive social relationships, (2) contribute to peer acceptance and friendship development, (3) result in satisfactory school management, and (4) allow individuals to cope with and adapt to the demands of the social environment" (p. 364).

Along with this definition, Gresham (1998) proposed a two-dimensional model of social skills and interfering problem behaviors in which social skills can be classified into three distinct classes: 1) social acquisition deficits; 2) social performance deficits; and 3) social fluency deficits.

Social acquisition deficits are defined as the absence of knowledge of how to execute particular social skills or a failure to discriminate when certain social behaviors are appropriate. Social performance deficits recognize the presence of a social skill or skills, but there is a failure to perform the acceptable behavior in specific situations. Social fluency deficits reflect the presence of a skill, but there is an inability to perform the skill because of a lack of appropriate models or practice, or inconsistent reinforcement when the skill is used.

These three classes enable us to assess youth behaviors and move toward determining an appropriate intervention. Also included in assessment is the determination of interfering problem behaviors, the second dimension of Gresham's two-dimensional model. Many times, youth have internalized or externalized problems, which compete or interfere with skill acquisition, performance, or fluency. This makes it necessary for recognition and intervention to occur simultaneously. Internal problem behaviors can be characterized as fear, social withdrawal, depression, etc. External problem behaviors can be characterized as impulsivity, aggression, hyperactivity, etc. (Gresham, 1998; Gresham, Van, & Cook, 2006).

Social competence is a judgment made by others that reflects one's ability to perform a social skill adequately and receive appropriate reinforcement. If we are to effectively teach youth appropriate alternative or replacement behaviors that ensure they receive ongoing reinforcement for recognizing, choosing, and using the right social skill, we must be able to identify and recognize factors that influence youths' performance of skills and allow them to be perceived as socially competent (Spence, 2003). These factors include the ability to...

■ Use interpersonal problem-solving skills.

■ Perceive and process social information.

■ Understand and choose the appropriate skill.

■ Manage emotions and affect while interacting with others.

■ Self-monitor and make adjustments to behavior as needed.

■ Understand and interpret any environmental contingencies that require the modification or adaptation of a skill.

These factors occur simultaneously and rapidly during any given interaction with others and are more reflexive than planned. Any part of an interaction that is planned reflects on a youth's ability to spontaneously solve problems and implement solutions immediately when appropriate reinforcement for the interaction is not obtained. This reflects the adjustments necessary during a sustained socially competent interaction. Addressing any competent social interaction requires knowledge, mastery, and fluency to be successful. Without these there will be misperception, misinterpretation, and possibly an escalation in negative behavior.

The philosophy of social skill instruction within Boys Town programs is that youth have strengths and weaknesses (identified problem behaviors), and that active, direct instruction and practice is a key to remediation and growth. Focusing on a youth's strengths provides a foundation and a starting place for building skills and alleviating weaknesses, and provides a positive approach to remediation and intervention. Positive, prosocial behaviors, including those that require growth, can be modeled, taught, and rewarded, and therefore, become viable alternatives for a youth who has gotten into trouble in such situations in the past.

Benefits of Social Skills Training

Social skills training has numerous benefits and ultimately can assist in developing social competence. Benefits include improving one's ability to get along with others, maintaining self-control, regulating affect, increasing academic success, and improving self-esteem, self-confidence, and self-efficacy. As noted earlier, interfering problem behaviors can hinder or block a youth's ability to achieve social competence. Numerous studies related to specific problem behaviors and the use of social skills training to address them indicate promise in helping youth improve or develop increased social competence. Areas where improvements have been noted include aggression, juvenile delinquency, child abuse and neglect, and mental health disorders.

A number of experts also have reported positive findings regarding the effect of social and emotional learning on student behavior and academic performance (Greenberg, Weissberg, O'Brien, Zins, Fredericks, Resnik, & Elias, 2003; Zins, Weissberg, Wang, & Walberg, 2004). A meta-analysis of 75 studies on social and emotional learning programs revealed positive outcomes in seven major areas: social skills, positive self-image, prosocial behavior, antisocial behavior, substance abuse, mental health, and academic achievement (Sklad, Diekstra, DeRitter, Ben, & Gravesteijn, 2012).

Another distinct advantage of social skills training is that it can be used as a primary, secondary, or tertiary intervention (Walker, Ramsey, & Gresham, 2004). As we examine in later chapters, varying interventions enables caregivers to do group and individual teaching and allows for general-to-specific intervention, based on the severity of the problem at hand.

Primary interventions are those that deal with teaching general social skills to larger groups of youth and do not target a specific skill for change. This intervention is focused more on developing and improving the overall positive climate of a program or classroom. A secondary intervention is more specific in its overall goal of dealing with youth who are having difficulties with a specific class or set of skills (e.g., self-control, problem-solving, etc.), and could benefit from focused social skills training. Many times, this intervention is done in small, homogenous groups, which creates more efficient and cost-effective teaching settings. Finally, tertiary interventions are focused on reducing negative, antisocial behavior that causes youth to be at risk for more restrictive interventions (e.g., foster care placement, incarceration, behavior programs, self-contained classrooms, etc.). This intervention requires more intensive individual services and generally requires specific treatment designs that focus on greatly reducing or eliminating antisocial behavior that, if left unchecked, will likely result in major life problems as a youth gets older.

Summary

Deficits in social functioning appear to be implicated in numerous behavioral problem areas that children, adolescents, and young adults face. While children of all ages can experience these deficits, developing the ability to interact effectively with others may be especially critical during adolescence. This is normally a time when a youth should be refining a variety of basic social behaviors and learning more complex skills necessary for the transition to adulthood (LeCroy, 1983; Ashford & LeCroy, 2013). Youth need to become increasingly skilled as they face the developmental tasks of adolescence, such as identity and value formation, independence from family, and appropriate group affiliation. Without a strong social and psychological base from which to develop, many adolescents fail to negotiate these tasks successfully.

Social skills training programs have repeatedly demonstrated their effectiveness in developing a wide range of interpersonal behaviors and skills in diverse populations of children and adolescents (Kazdin, 1985, 2001). The quality of any social skills training effort is enhanced by understanding and recognizing the complexity of social interactions, choosing appropriate social skills for normalizing those interactions, and teaching them in meaningful ways that can be valued by the youth, their peers, adults, and society in general. Caregivers can use group and individual interventions that are designed and structured to enhance interactions with their youth to build important life skills and treat behavioral deficits on a daily basis.

CHAPTER 2
Elements of Social Behavior

The goals of a social skills training program for youth are to establish new sets of responses to social situations and to teach youth how to integrate their behavior with others in the environment. In order to accomplish this, caregivers working with the youth must have a clear conception of what constitutes social behavior and social skills, as well as a method of analyzing youths' current level of functioning. This chapter focuses on the functional relationships between a youth's behavior and the environment, the structure of appropriate social skills and task analysis, and methods of assessing skill deficits and targeting alternative responses.

Functional Relationships of Behavior

A behavioral approach to social skills training first recognizes that all behaviors occur within a context of environmental events. A youth engages in a particular behavior or activity in a given situation in order to have some effect on their surroundings. Examples of this may include getting someone's attention, obtaining a possession, or being left alone. But the result of that behavior, whatever the original intent, also will have an effect on the youth. Thus, the relationship between a youth's behavior and the environment is

bi-directional, or functional. The youth is affecting the social environment, while the environment is simultaneously affecting the youth.

The events in the environment that may serve to modify or control a youth's responses are numerous but can be generalized into two main categories: antecedent events and consequent events. Both of these are closely associated in time with the occurrence of a behavior.

Antecedent Events

An antecedent event represents the situation or conditions that immediately precede a behavior or performance of a skill. Often, the antecedent event is a cue to a person that a particular behavior would be appropriate in that situation. For example, a ringing doorbell is a cue, or antecedent event, for going to the door and answering it.

Antecedent events are critical when attempting to analyze a problem behavior a youth is using. A caregiver (parent, youth-care worker, teacher, or counselor) may be able to examine the events that immediately precede a negative behavior, such as a tantrum or becoming physically aggressive, and begin to detect patterns in the behavior's occurrence. For example, a youth may begin to argue and whine when told "No," but not when he is asked to complete a chore. In this case, the antecedent event would indicate to the caregiver that more time should be spent teaching the youth the social skill of "Accepting 'No' for an Answer" and not as much time needs to be spent on teaching the skill of "Following Instructions." The pattern of antecedent events that may be observed around any particular behavior problem or skill deficit of a youth will help determine the appropriate alternative skill to teach.

It also should be mentioned that improvement in problem behaviors, as well as gains in social skills, can be accomplished through manipulation of antecedent events (Gresham, 1981; Gresham, Van, & Cook, 2006). If a parent complains that his son always loses his temper when told to go to bed, observation may reveal that the parent walks into the living room in the middle of a television show each night and commands the child to go to bed. Changing the antecedent event by having the parent prompt the child 15 minutes before bedtime that bedtime is approaching and negotiating a bedtime that is after the youth's television show may be enough to prevent the problem from occurring.

Recognizing antecedent events and choosing correct responses can be a major challenge for youth with social skill deficiencies. Situations that are ambiguous, including ones where others give vague verbal or nonverbal responses, can be easily distorted and misinterpreted by these youth. Confusion over intent in ambiguous situations has been viewed as a major precursor to aggressive acting out in some youth (Patterson, 1982, 1992; Dodge, Price, Bachorowski, & Newman, 1990). Therefore, one area of teaching that should not be ignored by caregivers who are attempting to improve their youths' social competency is the recognition of situational cues and the strategies for dealing with these cues when they can be confusing or easily misinterpreted.

Consequent Events

Consequent events (or consequences) are the outcomes that result after a particular behavior or skill has occurred. Broadly speaking, behavioral consequences can be classified into two general types: reinforcing and punishing. Reinforcing consequences invariably strengthen the behavior they follow, and punishing consequences weaken the behavior they follow.

Consequent events also must be analyzed when caregivers are attempting to decrease a problem behavior or increase a positive behavior. By acting without determining whether a consequence will be helpful or harmful in a given situation, caregivers could unintentionally or inadvertently reinforce and/or increase a negative behavior they are trying to decrease. For example, if parents respond to their child's tantrums by giving in to her demands for a possession, or by ignoring the child and not interacting with her, both responses may increase the likelihood that the child will throw a tantrum again in similar situations. And remember that the relationship between the child's behavior and the environment is bi-directional. So, if the parents' giving in or ignoring immediately stops the child's tantrum, they are more likely to respond in the same way in the future. This, in turn, increases the likelihood of even more tantrums because the child learns that she can get what she wants or can avoid her parents by using that behavior. Such is the nature of functional relationships.

On the other hand, identifying and using consequences that will consistently reinforce positive behaviors in the social environment will increase the frequency of the positive behaviors over time. In order to establish and maintain new social skills in a youth, a caregiver must reinforce a youth

Antecedent Event	Behavior	Consequent Event
Joaquin approaches an adult and asks to go outside and play. The adult says, "No, it's time to get started on your homework."	Joaquin begins to argue, raise his voice, curse, and complain that the adult is never fair to him.	The adult responds by saying, "Okay, you can go outside, but only for 20 minutes." Joaquin calms down immediately and goes outside to play.

Figure 1

anytime they use the skill, especially when first teaching the skill. When the youth becomes proficient at using the skill and begins to experience the natural reinforcement that results (e.g., comfort in social situations, better peer acceptance, more effective communication), the caregiver's rewarding of those behaviors becomes less important and can be faded out.

In conducting a functional analysis of a youth's social behavior, caregivers begin by observing and describing the antecedent and consequent events that appear to precede and follow each significant behavior. Between these two descriptions, caregivers can construct a detailed account of the youth's behavior. By analyzing each component (the "ABCs" – Antecedent, Behavior, Consequence), a caregiver should obtain a relatively clear picture of: 1) events that appear to be cues for the behavior to occur; 2) consequences that seem to be maintaining the behavior; and 3) the appropriate social skill that should be taught in order to replace the youth's current problem behavior. An example of a functional analysis is provided in Figure 1.

By analyzing this interaction according to a functional analysis model, we could obtain the following information:

1. The situational cue for Joaquin to begin arguing and cursing appears to be when he is denied a request (or told "No").

2. The consequent event that is likely to maintain the behavior is the adult giving in to Joaquin's arguing and complaints about fairness, and Joaquin engaging in an enjoyable activity immediately following the behavior.

3. The two skill areas that should be addressed in this situation are Joaquin's difficulty with accepting "No" answers and following instructions.

This example illustrates the information that can be obtained through a functional analysis exercise and observation of a youth's social behavior. The critical elements of any behavior pattern are the events that precede and follow the target behavior or skill, and the specific verbal and nonverbal components of the skill.

Social Skill Components

In a behavioral teaching program, it is important to distinguish between skills and the behaviors that are part of them. Behaviors are individual, discrete, observable acts demonstrated as part of a larger measure of activity. Some behaviors may be so subtle that they are performed unconsciously, such as looking at a person who is talking to you, and may be part of nearly every social skill.

Skills, on the other hand, are sets of related behaviors or components that are designed to produce positive results for the user in defined situations. It is the consistent and generalized use of such skills that constitute social competency (LeCroy, 1983; Ashford & LeCroy, 2013; Spence & Donovan, 1998). It is critical that caregivers become adept at defining, recognizing,

---

GUIDELINES FOR TASK ANALYSIS

1. The scope of the main task or skill should be kept limited.

2. Subtasks (behaviors) should be written in observable terms.

3. Terminology should be at a level understood by the potential user.

4. The task should be written in terms of what the learner will do.

5. The task, not the learner, should be the focus of attention.

(Moyer & Dardig, 1978)

Figure 2

teaching, and reinforcing the behavioral elements of social skills.

The elements of social skills are identified and defined through a process called "task analysis" (Cartledge & Milburn, 1995; Cartledge & Kleefeld, 2009). The essential steps involved in the task analysis of a social skill area are:

1. Specifying the desired outcome or goal

2. Identifying the essential component

behaviors of the goal or skill

3. Stating the behavioral elements of the skill in observable terms

4. Sequencing the component behaviors in order of performance

For example, if a desired outcome for a particular youth is stated as "will comply with instructions," the task analysis process might guide the caregiver to teach the youth to: 1) look at the person giving the instruction; 2) acknowledge that you heard the instruction; 3) get started right away and stay on task; and 4) let the person know when you are done.

It is important when task-analyzing social behavior to remember that the youth is the primary person who needs to comprehend the listing of individual behaviors. Therefore, the analysis of social skills, if it is to be an effective intervention tool and resource, must be concise and clear, and use objective language. Figure 2 summarizes guidelines for effective task analysis of social skills.

Deficits in social functioning can be measured and assessed in numerous ways. The primary methods of formal assessment, mainly in populations of younger children, include sociometric measures, naturalistic observation and recording, and teacher/caregiver ratings (Gresham, 1981; Gresham, Van, & Cook, 2006; Oden, 1980). These techniques are primarily designed to produce ratings of peer acceptance, popularity, and social integration that can be correlated with other characteristics of children who score particularly low or high on these measures.

Once skill deficits are observed and defined, caregivers can choose appropriate alternative skills to teach as substitutes. This is accomplished most effectively on an individual, prescriptive basis for each youth.

Replacement Skills for Conduct-Disordered Youth

Accepting Consequences

Accepting Criticism (Feedback)
or a Consequence

Accepting Decisions of Authority

Accepting "No" for an Answer

Being Assertive

Caring for the Property of Others

Communicating Honestly

Compromising with Others

Controlling Emotions

Controlling the Impulse to Steal

Coping with Anger and Aggression
from Others

Coping with Conflict

Dealing with an Accusation

Dealing with Frustration

Disagreeing Appropriately

Expressing Empathy and
Understanding for Others

Expressing Feelings Appropriately

Following Instructions

Following Rules

Getting the Teacher's Attention

Interrupting Appropriately

Keeping Property in Its Place

Listening to Others

Making an Apology

Making New Friends

Making Positive Statements
about Others

Making Restitution (Compensating)

Negotiating with Others

Problem-Solving a Disagreement

Seeking Positive Attention

Showing Respect

Showing Sensitivity to Others

Using Anger Control (Self-Control)
Strategies

Using Appropriate Language

Using Relaxation Strategies

Using Self-Monitoring and
Self-Reflection

Using Structured Problem-Solving
(SODAS)

Waiting Your Turn

Figure 3

However, some generalities can be made in order to demonstrate how the choice of opposite competing skills is targeted. Sterba and Dowd (1998) identified a list of possible replacement skills that could be taught as part of intervention for conduct-disordered youth. Their list is summarized in Figure 3.

The process of developing skill-based interventions for youth with difficult behavioral problems is initially dependent on the caregiver's ability to clearly specify and target areas that need remediation and frequent teaching. Agreement then needs to be reached regarding what skills constitute "behavioral opposites" and how they will be taught. For example, if one youth accompanies another in a shoplifting episode, and some caregivers are teaching the skill of "Communicating Honestly" while others are teaching "Resisting Peer Pressure," the youth may not receive the intended benefits in either area

Summary

The fundamental elements of a youth's social behavior and skills include the context or situational variables in which they occur, the behavioral components that the youth is capable of performing, and the consequent events that affect future performance. Also, in order for most youth to become socially "competent," they need to be capable of recognizing the subtle social cues of others in the course of an interaction and making appropriate behavioral adjustments. This is a particular challenge for youth diagnosed with Autism Spectrum Disorder. Though recognition of subtle social cues is a challenge for these youth, teaching them the social skills necessary to succeed in life is one way to help them work around these challenges.

In Boys Town programs, our comprehensive Social Skills Curriculum guides staff members' instructional interactions and service planning. This Curriculum is presented in Chapter 7. Each skill is task-analyzed and later grouped according to related behavior problem areas and relevant situations (see Appendices C and D) in order to augment the service planning process for serious youth issues or special populations.

CHAPTER 3
Individual Teaching Techniques

When teaching skills to children and adolescents, how the skills are taught is often as important as what is being taught. In other words, caregivers must have an effective, structured method for helping youth learn new skills, improve on existing skills, and become proficient at choosing the right skills to use in specific situations.

The teaching methods that are covered in this chapter are integral parts of the Boys Town Model® and are effective in helping children and youth build a repertoire of skills in a variety of settings. By using components such as modeling, demonstration, role-playing, giving feedback, practice, and activities to promote generalization, these teaching approaches work together to prevent inappropriate youth behavior, reinforce positive behavior, and correct negative behavior.

Many children who lack critical skills may not have had the benefit of growing up in an environment where positive social behavior was taught or reinforced. The adults present may not have modeled appropriate styles of interacting with others and the local peer culture or neighborhood may not have valued these positive behaviors. A child, therefore, may not have received any direct instruction in appropriate ways to get their immediate needs fulfilled, as is typical in most functional family settings (Oden, 1980).

The lack of reinforcement for important social skills may be a particularly critical feature in the learning histories of children with serious behavioral and emotional problems. For example, Patterson (1982, 1992) and his colleagues found that parents of children who were later described as having aggressive behavior problems were more likely to: 1) use harsh commands and demands with their children; 2) reward negative behaviors with attention or compliance; and 3) ignore, or even punish, prosocial behaviors that their children demonstrated at home. New data point to other negative or antisocial behavior on the part of parents, as well. These children, then, are more likely to act out aggressively in conflict situations at school and with peers, and to be deficient in critical social skill areas such as compliance with rules, problem-solving strategies, and communication skills. While one task of the caregiver – child care service provider, educator, parent, etc. – may be confronting inappropriate behaviors that occur, another simultaneous task is to encourage and motivate the child to replace those behaviors with more socially adaptive responses.

Before we review the teaching methods, let's look at two factors that set up successful teaching: specifying behaviors and identifying what skills to teach.

Specifying Behaviors

A key ingredient in any instructional interaction with a child is being specific. This means that behaviors and skills that are being taught are clearly defined, and even demonstrated for the child, reducing the potential for confusion as much as possible. Chapter 2 referred to the specific elements of appropriate social behavior and task analysis. This same degree of being specific and objective must be reflected in the verbal interactions between adults and the youth they work with or care for.

There are numerous advantages to teaching social skills in a clear, concrete manner. The overall effectiveness of an adult's instruction increases dramatically as the language used becomes more specific and objective. Youth are more likely to learn the components of social skills and, once learned, are more likely to generalize those skills to other situations in which it would be appropriate to use them (school, home, on the job, etc.). This may be particularly critical for youth who have cognitive or learning problems. For example, a learning-disabled child may have particular difficulty understanding vague instructions from teachers or caregivers, recognizing and interpreting the social cues of others, and choosing the appropriate social response in a given situation (Cruickshank, Morse, & Johns, 1980; McPhail, 1993). Clear descriptions and demonstrations of behaviors and skills may help these youth learn more efficiently and, subsequently, handle difficult or ambiguous social situations more successfully.

The process of describing skill components specifically and objectively also may enhance the quality of adult-youth relationships and build trust. Many youth, especially those receiving intervention services or in out-of-home placement, have been told repeatedly what not to do or have been "put down" for the problems they may have. But when adults take the time to instruct youth in a positive, objective manner, focusing on the skills to use in situations that have caused them difficulties in the past, they are communicating care and concern for the youth in a tangible way. As a result, the youth become more open to the adults' teaching and intervention and are more likely to try out the new skills and behaviors they have been taught. This is especially true when adults are careful to avoid judgmental and value-laden words ("that was wrong," "bad," "stupid," or "terrible") that may emotionally harm a child or trigger a negative reaction.

Identifying What Skills to Teach

The practical application of individual teaching techniques for building skills begins with identifying what skills should be taught to a youth. In terms of content and sequencing, individual teaching sessions can focus on: 1) a progression of skills from basic to more advanced; 2) skills specifically identified to be relevant to the youth's most critical issues or support needs; 3) preparation for a specific set of circumstances or event; or 4) all of the above. An important consideration in this process is that the youth begins to see the value in the skills that are to be taught (LeCroy, 1983; Ashford & LeCroy, 2013). If the youth sees appropriate skills as meaningful only to the adults who are teaching them, they are much less likely to internalize and generalize those skills. That is why it is so critical that the teaching process that is used to train the youth in a new set of skills includes steps that explain the personal benefits of learning such skills.

For the most part, the choice of which particular skills to teach a youth varies with the youth's immediate needs and long-term service goals (if applicable). Also, skills and teaching methods should always be appropriate for a child's age and developmental level. Once the skills have been identified and prioritized, an adult can map out a strategy that defines how best to teach necessary skills, reinforce their use, and promote internalization and generalization for long-term benefits.

Opportunities for Teaching and Reinforcing Skills

In almost every child care or educational setting, there are essentially three situations in which skill instruction takes place. They are:

■ When a youth is observed using a skill appropriately (or using an approximation of a skill)

■ When preparing or reminding a youth to use a skill in an upcoming situation

■ When a youth's inappropriate behavior must be corrected and an alternative appropriate behavior must be taught

The three teaching methods – Effective Praise, Proactive Teaching, and Corrective Teaching – highlighted in the next few pages have been developed to meet the needs of youth and those adults who work with youth in these situations. The beauty of these methods is that they can be modified and adapted to meet the needs of almost any youth in almost any situation and in almost any setting – schools, shelters, residential programs, intervention facilities, foster care homes, private care programs, and others.

While these methods are essential in providing structure for teaching to youth, there will always be times when informal teaching occurs. Teaching through modeling appropriate behaviors, discussing with youth events where someone used either an appropriate or an inappropriate behavior, and having informal conversations about routine matters all are opportunities for caregivers to help youth expand, enhance, and strengthen their skill base.

Effective Praise

Everyone likes praise. We want people to tell us when they notice we've done something well or accomplished a goal. Getting a pat on the back or a word of congratulations makes us feel good, both about what we've done and who we are.

This is especially true for children. Whether it's coloring a picture, studying hard for a test, or holding the door open for someone at the grocery store, kids love it when an adult notices they've used or tried to use a positive behavior.

Some of the children with whom you work may rarely have heard those important words of encouragement and praise. They may have been bombarded with feedback plenty of times, and at times, may have been physically punished for their misdeeds. And the times when these kids have tried to do the right thing or have found success, it may have been ignored or treated like it's nothing special.

The children in your care may be hungry for praise. As an important part of working with children, praise nurtures emotional growth and provides motivation for youngsters to learn new skills. It is also one of the key elements to building a warm, healthy relationship with kids. Giving praise shows that you genuinely care, that you will take the time to notice when a girl or boy does well, and that you are proud of each child's accomplishments and efforts. Consistently "catching 'em being good" also builds self-confidence in youth, enhances learning, and helps kids to like themselves. Eventually, youth begin to realize that they should use certain behaviors and skills simply because it's the right thing to do.

The best kind of praise is praise that is sincere, natural, and effective. By sincere we mean that youth understand that you are giving praise because you are pleased with what they've done, not just because it's part of your job or because you want them to do something. Praising children naturally means responding spontaneously in a positive way as part of your life. Sometimes, caregivers mistakenly think that praise situations have to be planned out, or that they are "episodes" that are separate from the daily routine. When that happens, caregivers can come across as "mechanical" and children don't see the praise as being sincere. The way to measure praise's effectiveness is by watching whether a child who is praised for a specific behavior continues to use the behavior. If they do, it's a good indicator that praise motivates the child and that they will try to repeat the behavior because it earns a positive response.

Although frequent general praise creates a nurturing atmosphere, there are times when praise needs to be more specific. (By general praise, we mean brief comments or statements – "Nice job!" "Way to go!" "All right!" – that adults use to informally recognize a youth's appropriate behavior.) At Boys Town, we've developed a teaching approach called Effective Praise, a step-by-step method to ensure that youth get clear messages about their positive be-

havior. Effective Praise is a way for caregivers to let youth know exactly what they did and why they should continue it, and then to give a positive consequence.

Steps of Effective Praise

Effective Praise has five steps. All caregivers should use all five steps when they first start working with youth. Later on, as caregivers become more comfortable with giving praise in this manner and have made it a natural part of their everyday contact with youth, a step or two may be left out. The point to remember when using Effective Praise is that praise must be sincere, and children must understand why they are being praised.

The five steps are:

1. **Give brief praise** – Offer short, enthusiastic words or expressions of praise that let the child know that you recognize they have done something well.

2. **Describe or demonstrate the appropriate behavior** – Specifically describe what the youth did, and if the situation calls for it, label the skill they used (followed instructions, greeted someone, accepted a "No" answer).

3. **Provide a rationale (reason) for using the behavior** – This helps children make the connection between what they say or do and the possible outcomes or results of their actions.

4. **Ask for acknowledgment** – Make sure the youth understands the reason for using the behavior and why they should continue using it. Depending on the setting, this acknowledgment may be as simple as eye contact, a head nod, or may be verbal.

5. **Give a positive consequence** – The youth earns a positive consequence,

which usually is some kind of reward; again, label the skill and specifically describe the behaviors as you tell the youth what they earned. **NOTE:** This step may be optional, depending on the setting and level of support a child needs. A more skilled child may not require a positive consequence, as the verbal praise may be reinforcement enough. A child who is low on skill mastery or highly externally motivated will likely require a positive consequence.

Here's what Effective Praise might sound like when a caregiver in a shelter program sees that a youth has followed an instruction to clean off the dinner table.

1. **Give brief praise** – *"All right! Look at this guy go."*

2. **Describe or demonstrate the appropriate behavior** – *"Jimmy, you did a great job of following instructions. You not only cleaned off all the dishes and silverware and took them to the sink, but you also put the leftovers in the refrigerator. And you did that on your own."*

3. **Provide a rationale (reason) for using the behavior** – *"When you follow instructions to complete chores like this, it helps keep the kitchen in order and shows us that we can count on you to take on responsibilities."*

4. **Ask for acknowledgment** – *"Do you understand why it's good for you to follow instructions when something needs to be done?"*

5. **Give a positive consequence** – *"Thanks for your help. For cleaning off the table and putting away the leftovers, you've earned a half hour of playing video games tonight."*

Here's another example that shows how Effective Praise can be adapted for different settings and situations. In this example, a teacher praises a usually shy fourth-grade student for participating in a class discussion.

1. **Give brief praise** – *"Portia, I wanted to let you know that I was very pleased with your participation in class today."*

2. **Describe the appropriate behavior** – *"You raised your hand almost every time I asked a question, and when I called on you, you gave clear answers that were full of good information."*

3. **Provide a rationale (reason) for using the behavior** – *"When you participate in class like that, you help yourself and the other students learn. And you show that you are paying attention and really thinking about what we are discussing."*

4. **Ask for acknowledgment** – *"Does that make sense?"*

5. **Give a positive consequence** – *"Great job in class today! For participating so well, you can help me hand out the markers and paper during art hour."*

As well as Effective Praise works, it should not totally take the place of more general praise that can be given anytime. Simply telling youth, "That's great," "Good job," or "Wonderful work," can go a long way toward letting them know their efforts are recognized and appreciated. This is especially true when youth use a specific skill or behavior frequently. When kids know they're doing something correctly and seem pleased with themselves for doing it, a simple "Thanks" may be all that is necessary to acknowledge the positive behavior.

31

When to Use Effective Praise

Sometimes, the hardest part about using Effective Praise is remembering to do it and remembering to do it often. Unfortunately, our society "trains" people to focus on the negative aspects of a situation rather than the positive. An example of this is what is known in the restaurant business as the "3-11" rule. This rule states that if you have a good dining experience, you will tell three people about it, but if you have a bad dining experience, you will tell 11 people. In other words, we tend to emphasize the negative over the positive.

It is easy to see when someone makes a mistake or does something wrong. But as a caregiver working with children who have not learned the "right" way to do many things, it is just as important to praise positive behavior as it is to correct negative behavior. Focusing your attention on what a child does well or their attempts to do the right thing may require you to change some of your behaviors and attitudes. This is yet another challenge of working with children.

At Boys Town, we have discovered a simple truth – praise works wonders. But some adults say that even when they praise children, it doesn't seem to work. Usually, we find that these adults are praising only the biggest achievements or momentous occasions. Once they begin to consistently notice and praise the little things, as well as the big things, their children are doing, they begin to see positive behavior changes. Never underestimate the power of praise.

This raises the question: Should we praise children for every positive behavior, even what they are supposed to do? The answer is "Yes." Children like praise, and the more often they receive it for even the simplest tasks – putting their clothes in the laundry basket, turning off the lights when they leave a room, bringing in the mail – the more likely they are to repeat those activities. Praise feeds a child's desire to succeed. Here are three areas to concentrate on when deciding what you should praise:

- **When youth use behaviors they already do well or that you want them to continue to use.** Often, adults don't see any reason to praise youth for things they do right; kids are just expected to make appropriate choices. However, it is not always easy for kids to make good decisions; when it happens, it is an extremely positive accomplishment. Giving credit for a child's success to their own effort and ability, and providing encouragement that similar success can be expected in the future, can give that child something to be proud of, even when they miss the mark while attempting new skills.

- **Improvements in behavior, even small ones.** Improvements worthy of praise might include a youth who normally argues and refuses to follow instructions; however, when given an instruction, this time he sighs and completes the instruction right away. This behavior demonstrates an improvement from what has been his usual response to an instruction and, therefore, warrants praise and recognition.

- **When youth are learning new skills and making positive attempts to use them.** Provide reinforcement every time a child uses a new skill correctly. This can help kids develop skills more quickly and increase the probability that they will use those skills again. Don't be surprised if kids become frustrated the first few times they try to use a new skill. This is natural. (Think about the first time you tried to begin an exercise or diet program, repair a broken appliance, or wallpaper a room.) That's why kids need a great deal of encouragement. Once a new skill is learned and mastered, the amount of encouragement can be reduced.

It is sometimes very difficult for children to learn new skills. When they try to learn something new, praise the effort. Enthusiastically praising positive attempts to learn or try new skills and make other improvements will carry over to many other areas of children's lives. Make the most of every opportunity to praise kids' positive attempts to learn.

Effective Praise is a teaching tool that recognizes and rewards youth for using skills and specific positive behaviors, increasing the likelihood that they will use those behaviors in the future. Praise helps build positive relationships with kids, while helping them to begin feeling good about themselves and their accomplishments. When Effective Praise is used frequently, kids will become more positive and be more receptive to your teaching and/or intervention.

Proactive Teaching

Is it better to correct and teach a child not to touch a hot stove after she has burned her hand on it, or to teach her ahead of time that touching a hot stove can hurt her and she shouldn't go near it?

Obviously, teaching a child how to prevent or avoid a potentially harmful situation would be better than letting the child get hurt before teaching takes place. When it comes to preparing and helping children

learn how to respond to the many situations they will face, prevention is the key! This is the idea behind the Boys Town method called Proactive Teaching (sometimes referred to as Preventive Teaching).

Proactive Teaching is a way for adults to introduce new skills, reinforce skills youth are learning, and to prepare youth for future situations where they will need to use certain skills or behaviors. This is similar to how a coach prepares his team or players for an upcoming game. This teaching occurs during planned, neutral times, when kids are not upset or being corrected, and when the adult (parent, teacher, staff member, etc.) and the youth can both concentrate on what is being taught and learned.

Proactive Teaching is so important to the care and development of children because, as we have said, many youth have not yet learned even the basic skills that are needed to function and be successful in society. Normally, children begin learning these basic skills – "Following Instructions," "Getting Along with Others," "Accepting 'No' for an Answer," "Accepting Criticism (Feedback) or a Consequence," and others – at an early age from their parents and other significant adults in their lives. Adult caretakers model certain behaviors, show and tell children how to do skills and when to use them, and continually help children practice, either formally or informally, to help them get better at using those skills.

Many kids don't always have those invaluable learning experiences. They may not know things like how to solve problems without getting angry, how to ask for something politely, or how to share. These skill deficits often have landed them in trouble and have added to the frustration and anger they feel when they are not able to get what they want or need, or accomplish a goal.

In addition to introducing new skills and reinforcing ones that youth already know how to do, Proactive Teaching is vital in helping children achieve "generalization." Generalization, a skill in itself, is the ability to adapt a specific skill to a variety of antecedents, situations, or circumstances. (See Chapter 4 for more on generalization.) For example, a youth who can proficiently use the skill of "Following Instructions" at home, at school, and at swimming practice has learned how to "generalize" the skill to different situations and people. As caregivers, the ultimate goal is for kids to be able to think for themselves, make good decisions, and follow through with appropriate, prosocial behaviors, **on their own.** Proactive Teaching is the training ground where children learn how to do that.

As with all our teaching methods, Proactive Teaching should become a natural part of the care you provide for children. An adult's biggest challenge here is to recognize what needs to be taught, when it needs to be taught, how best to teach it, and how to determine whether a youth is learning.

The Steps of Proactive Teaching

Proactive Teaching has seven steps. When it is first used with new youth and with youth who are learning new skills, all seven steps should be used in each teaching session. As youth become more skilled, adults may choose to modify their teaching to fit a child's individual needs and situation. This might mean briefer teaching sessions because youth are already familiar with a skill and are getting better at using it. The steps are listed here and an explanation and example follows.

1. **Give initial praise.**
2. **Identify the skill and give examples.**

3. **Describe or demonstrate the appropriate behavior (give the skill steps).**
4. **Provide a rationale (reason) and request acknowledgment.**
5. **Practice.**
    * Give feedback.
    * Issue a positive consequence.
6. **Schedule a follow-up practice.**
7. **Offer praise and encouragement throughout.**

1. **Give initial praise.**

The best way to begin a teaching session is on a positive note. Specifically and sincerely praise any aspect of a child's behavior that is appropriate to the situation. Starting the teaching positively establishes an atmosphere where the child is more likely to listen, participate, and learn.

Example: *"Thanks for taking a few minutes to talk with me, Sanjay."*

2. **Identify the skill and give examples.**

Begin the next step by clearly labeling and explaining the skill. Review a number of specific ways the skill can be used and give the youth plenty of opportunities to ask clarifying questions. Also describe how the skill can be used in a variety of situations and settings; this shows the child that it can be applied in many conditions or settings.

Example: *"Sanjay, I want to talk with you about a skill that will really help you here while you're in this program, at home, on the job, and in school. It's called 'Following Instructions.' You may get instructions from staff members here and from your teachers at school. And when you go home, I'm sure your mom will have instructions she will want you to follow."*

3. **Describe or demonstrate the appropriate behavior (give the skill steps).**

In this step, specifically describe the behaviors that make up the skill. Demonstrating the skill is a good way to describe it, and a demonstration may be necessary for younger children or youth at lower developmental levels.

Example: *"When someone gives you an instruction, Sanjay, you should look at the person and, with a pleasant voice, say something like 'Okay' or 'Sure.' Then, do the task right away. When you're done, check back with the person by saying something like 'Okay, I'm done. Is there anything else?' That would be the best way to follow instructions."*

Again, you might need to demonstrate the skill to ensure that the youth understands. Demonstrations are especially helpful in communicating body posture, voice tone, facial expressions, and other behaviors that are difficult to describe verbally.

4. **Provide a rationale (reason) and request acknowledgment.**

A rationale for learning the skill is next, along with a request for a verbal acknowledgment from the youth. Here, you are asking the youth if they understand why it is important to use the particular skill.

Example: *"Sanjay, when you are able to follow instructions from staff members, teachers, or your parents really well, you may have more time to do the things you want to do. Do you understand?"*

5. **Practice (give feedback and a positive consequence).**

After describing the behavior and providing a rationale, have the youth practice the skill. Practicing helps youth become more comfortable with the skill and allows adults to determine the clarity and quality of their teaching up to this point. After the youth practices, provide feedback in the form of sincere, descriptive praise for all

appropriate behaviors, along with a positive consequence for the practice session. Just like Effective Praise, this step may be optional, depending on the setting or program. A more generalized setting, such as a general education classroom or at home, may not involve a positive consequence. However, a child requiring a more supportive intervention or setting may earn positive consequences for practicing.

Example:

Staff member: *"Let's practice just to make sure you got it. Let's pretend I'm your mom at home. When I give you an instruction, look at me, say, 'Okay, I'll get on that,' pretend to do the task, then let me know you are done. Are you ready?"*

Staff member (playing Mom): *"Sanjay, will you go finish cleaning your room?"*

Sanjay: *"Okay, I'll get on that right now."* [Sanjay pretends to clean room.] *"I'm done with my room. Is there anything else?"*

Staff member: *"Fantastic! When I gave you that instruction, you looked at me, used a pleasant voice tone, and said, 'Okay, I'll get on that right now.' Then, you pretended to do the task and checked back with me when you were done. You have done an outstanding job of practicing and learning the new skill of 'Following Instructions'! For practicing the skill, you have earned a positive consequence of having an extra snack."*

6. **Schedule a follow-up practice.**

Teaching is further reinforced through a series of follow-up practice sessions. Ideally, the first practice should occur shortly after the teaching session (5 to 15 minutes). Other practices can be done later in the day or evening.

Example: *"It's important that we practice the skill of 'Following Instructions' again real soon. Let's practice in about 15 minutes, okay?"*

To further help the youth succeed in these follow-up sessions, prompt them before the extra practice. The prompt reminds the child of the skill that was practiced earlier and may include having them briefly describe the appropriate behaviors that make up the skill. After each practice, continue to provide descriptive praise, descriptions of the appropriate behavior, and positive consequences. Over time, prompts can be faded out as youth show that they can remember and demonstrate the skill consistently.

7. Offer praise and encouragement throughout.

Throughout your teaching it is important to provide specific, ongoing praise to the youth. The teaching should end as it began – positively – with praise for the youth's participation and recognition of the appropriate behaviors the youth displayed during the interaction.

Example: *"Thanks for taking the time to practice with me. You looked at me during the entire session, stayed on task, and asked some good questions to help you understand what I meant."*

Preventive Prompt

Another type of Proactive Teaching is the preventive prompt. A preventive prompt is a brief reminder or statement about the use of a skill just before a situation in which the child will use the skill. This is like a coach reminding one of her players about how to run a specific play before sending the player into a game. An adult can use visual, verbal, or physical cues to remind youth what skill they are expected to use and to provide encouragement and reinforcement. A good example of a preventive prompt would be asking a youth, "Do you remember the steps to following instructions?" just before asking him to empty the dishwasher. Preventive prompts are a quick, easy way to help children remember appropriate behaviors and prevent inappropriate behaviors.

When to Use Proactive Teaching

Proactive Teaching can be done privately with one youth or in small groups. Adults can focus on teaching basic social skills or advanced treatment-oriented skills, preparing a youth for a specific set of circumstances, or "troubleshooting" a youth's skill deficits. When you first begin working with a youth, there should be a heavy emphasis on Proactive Teaching. However, we encourage adults to continue to use this teaching technique whenever necessary.

In settings ranging from schools to residential care, one of the first Proactive Teaching sessions might include teaching youth rules and routines, how they work, and why they are important. Early sessions also can focus on an explanation of the basic skills that are needed to be successful in a program, at school, within one's family, and in one's community.

Once this basic information is communicated to a youth, the youth can be introduced to skills that have been identified as ones that they need to learn or work on. As mentioned earlier, basic skills usually are taught first. Examples of basic skills to be taught include "Following Instructions," "Accepting Criticism (Feedback) or a Consequence," "Accepting 'No' for an Answer," "Accepting Consequences," "Making a Request (Asking a Favor)," and "Disagreeing Appropriately." Proactively teaching these basic skills helps the youth become more open to and comfortable with the process of learning new skills. These basic skills should be taught to every child; they are the building blocks to successfully learning advanced skills.

Often, the process of learning new skills is reinforcing in and of itself, both for youth and adults. In effect, it is easier to teach youth once they've acquired the basic skills.

Most children receive a gradual education in basic and advanced skills from their parents and other adults through modeling, discussion, praise, and discipline. But as we mentioned earlier, many youth have not been part of this natural, prosocial education process. In fact, these youth may have received an inconsistent and often dysfunctional education that has left them confused and socially inept. Frequent, specific Proactive Teaching is critical if these youngsters are to make up for lost time and lost opportunities.

Caregivers also can use Proactive Teaching when they are helping with a specific skill or behavior that is giving a youth problems. Often, this type of skill deficit can escalate and lead to a loss of self-control. Proactive Teaching can help reduce the chances of an emotional response. For example, if a youth consistently becomes verbally or physically aggressive and loses self-control when given a "No" answer, Proactive Teaching sessions should focus on the skill of "Accepting 'No' for an Answer."

Proactive Teaching builds relationships and fosters skill development. It can be used to teach youth basic and advanced social skills, prepare youth for specific situations or circumstances, and "troubleshoot" specific skill deficiencies. Proactive Teaching can be done on an individual basis or with the entire group of youth, depending on the circumstances. Proactive Teaching is a real key to youth success and to a caregiver's sense of accomplishment.

Corrective Teaching

While an important goal is to praise children for using appropriate skills and behaviors whenever possible, and to prepare them for situations where they will have to use certain skills, there will be times when you have to correct a child's misbehavior.

As a caregiver or teacher, you are responsible for helping children learn new appropriate behaviors and skills that can be used to replace past problem behaviors. These new skills assist younger children in their normal development as they grow through adolescence, and help adolescents as they grow into adulthood. When kids are directly and consistently taught new ways of behaving, they can more successfully and comfortably adapt to societal norms and get their needs met in more acceptable ways.

Direct, frequent, consistent, and concerned teaching also helps caregivers. A structured teaching approach provides a specific, effective, and positive way to deal with problem behaviors. Because teaching is a positive intervention that works well and is better received by children, you can avoid punitive approaches that would damage relationships.

At Boys Town, we have developed a teaching method called Corrective Teaching for dealing with problem behaviors and teaching more appropriate replacement behaviors. By thoughtfully and consistently using Corrective Teaching, you can help each child recover from the past and grow into the future.

Steps of Corrective Teaching

Corrective Teaching consists of a series of eight brief steps characterized by three central concepts – description, relationship, and consequence. Description involves specifically describing a behavior through words or actions, role-playing, and practice. The relationship concept involves using warmth and pleasantness, and showing genuine concern for the youth. It also focuses on helping the child learn how to develop healthy relationships with others. Consequences include giving feedback and practice, and having a youth lose a privilege or something they like for using an inappropriate behavior. For teaching to be effective, there must be a balance among these three concepts.

Let's take a closer look at the steps and their definitions:

1. **Give initial praise or empathy.**

2. **Describe or demonstrate the inappropriate behavior.**

3. **Issue a negative consequence.**
   * Positive correction statement

4. **Describe or demonstrate the appropriate behavior (give the skill steps).**

5. **Provide a rationale (reason) and request acknowledgment.**

6. **Practice.**

7. **Give feedback.**
   * Praise
   * Positive consequence (up to half of the negative consequence)

8. **Offer praise and encouragement throughout.**

1. **Give initial praise or empathy.**

This begins teaching on a positive note. Using a statement of empathy (e.g., "I know this is hard for you.") lets kids know you care and want to help. Praise statements (e.g., "Thanks for coming over right away to talk with me.") recognize the child for using a positive behavior. Both kinds of statements are excellent ways to prevent a youngster from reacting with volatile behaviors to your upcoming teaching and consequence.

2. **Describe or demonstrate the inappropriate behavior.**

The description of what the child did incorrectly should be simple and brief so that the child can understand it. For some kids, especially younger children and youth at lower developmental levels, a demonstration may be necessary. A word of caution: Spending too much time on the description of the misbehavior can come across as "nagging," which can trigger a loss of self-control from youngsters.

3. **Issue a negative consequence.**

This step involves having a youth lose something that is meaningful to them for using the inappropriate behavior. When consequences are issued, it is important children understand that their behavior earned the consequence and they are responsible for that behavior. After the consequence is issued, tell the child they will have a chance to earn back part of the consequence (no more than half) for practicing an alternative appropriate skill with you. This is called a "positive correction statement," and it gives kids hope that all is not lost. Positive correction can help give youth, who may have difficulty accepting correction, incentive to remain compliant through the teaching conversation.

4. **Describe or demonstrate the appropriate behavior (give the skill steps).**

In this step, give a simple and brief explanation of the skill or behavior the youngster should use in place of the inappropriate behavior. If necessary, go over the steps to a specific skill or demonstrate the specific behavior you want the youth to use in a similar situation. You also can help the youth generalize the skill or behavior to other situations by saying something like, "When an adult you know and trust asks you to [name the skill or behavior], you should...." Again, it is important to make sure your words or demonstration match the child's age and developmental level.

5. Provide a rationale (reason) and request acknowledgement.

This step is when you tell youth why they should change their behavior. In a sense, it's where you "sell" the skill to kids. Generally speaking, younger children and kids who are new to teaching respond best to rationales that let them know the personal benefits of using the new behavior. A rationale that explains the negative consequences of continuing to use the old inappropriate behavior also works with these kids. With older youth and youngsters who are familiar with your teaching, "other-centered" rationales usually work best. These rationales let kids know how using a new skill or behavior will benefit others. Here, caregivers are helping kids move away from thinking only of themselves to thinking about how their behaviors and actions affect others. As a result, kids begin to learn and develop morals and positive values.

After giving a rationale, ask youth if they understand it and what is being taught. If a child doesn't understand the rationale, patiently provide another one. It's important not to move on to the next step until the child lets you know that they understand what you are teaching. Requests for ac-

knowledgment can be used anytime during teaching when a youth appears confused.

6. Practice.

Here, the youth is given an opportunity to use the new skill or behavior in a pretend situation. Make sure to set up the practice clearly so they aren't confused about what to do. The best practices are ones that are somehow related to the child's original inappropriate behavior. (Avoid practices that might come across as contrived or silly; for example, don't say, "Jalen, please pick up that pencil," when practicing the skill of "Following Instructions" because Jalen didn't take out the garbage when asked.) Practice is important because it gives the child a chance to be successful and gain confidence before they have to use the skill or behavior in a real-life situation.

7. Give feedback.

Following the practice, tell the youth how well they did using the new behavior or skill. This provides an opportunity for youth to "fine-tune" their new behaviors and skills. Depending on the situation, you may have the youth practice again or simply point out anything that was left out and remind them to include it the next time the skill is used. After the practice and feedback, kids can earn back up to half of the negative consequence (positive correction) given earlier. For example, if a youth's consequence is losing a half hour of playing outside, they could earn back a maximum of 15 minutes of playing outside for practicing and accepting feedback. Positive correction is a powerful incentive for getting kids to take practicing seriously and not give up when the negative consequence is delivered.

8. Offer praise and encouragement throughout.

This ends teaching on a positive note by recognizing and praising a youngster's efforts to learn and practice a new behavior. Praising and encouraging kids at this time and throughout the interaction helps take their focus away from the negative consequence and allows them to leave the teaching session feeling good about themselves.

Corrective Teaching Example

Let's take a look at two examples of what Corrective Teaching might look and sound like when teaching the skills of "Ignoring Distractions" and "Accepting 'No' for an Answer." The first example occurs in a self-contained classroom that uses a motivation system, while the second example occurs in a more generalized environment.

Scenario: Malika and Marlon are students in a self-contained classroom that uses point cards to guide the use of consequences as part of a motivation system. While the teacher was redirecting Malika on her behavior, Marlon interrupted their conversation by commenting about the correction Malika received. Marlon said, *"Damn, she told you!"* Marlon's words cued the teacher to begin Corrective Teaching with him.

Teacher:

Step 1: Give praise or empathy.

"Marlon, I know it's hard to focus when there is a lot going on around you."

Step 2: Describe or demonstrate the inappropriate behavior.

"Just now, as I was working with Malika, I heard you say some words to her."

Step 3: Issue a negative consequence along with a positive correction statement.

"For not ignoring distractions, you have lost a thousand points on your point card. But remember, if you can focus now and work with me, you'll have a chance to earn half of those points back. Let's go ahead and write a negative one thousand points on your card for failing to ignore distractions." [Marlon writes the points on his card.] *"Good job of listening and following instructions. Thank you."* [Use praise throughout.]

Step 4: Describe or demonstrate the appropriate behavior (give the skill steps).

"Remember, when it's 'Focus Time' you're expected to use the skill of 'Ignoring Distractions.' That means not looking at the person who's distracting you, staying focused on your work, and not responding to any of the person's behaviors."

Step 5: Provide a rationale (reason) and request acknowledgement.

"Ignoring distractions and focusing on your work will keep you from falling behind and help you stay out of trouble. Does that make sense?"

Step 6: Practice.

"So let's try this again. I'm going to finish working with Malika. While I'm doing that, I'll be watching to see if you stay quiet and keep focused on your assignment."

[The teacher can return to her conversation with Malika while observing Marlon's behavior. After a few minutes, the teacher can return to Marlon and finish Corrective Teaching. If necessary, the teacher can go back and finish her conversation with Malika.]

Step 7: Give feedback, praise, and a positive consequence.

"Marlon, nice job of working quietly. When I was across the room, I saw you were focused on your assignment and your voice was off. For ignoring distractions, let's go ahead and get some positive points on your card under the skill of 'Ignoring Distractions.' That will be 500 points, and please mark that 'PC' for positive correction."

Step 8: Offer praise and encouragement.

"I'll go ahead and sign your card. Thanks for doing such a great job of cooperating. Now let's get back to work."

Our next example shows what Corrective Teaching might look and sound like when teaching the skill of "Accepting 'No' for an Answer" in a more generalized setting (at home, an afterschool program, a group home, or other similar environments). These settings may not use a specific motivation system for consequences or have the structure of a more specialized environment. Regardless, Corrective Teaching can be used just as effectively. In this example, a logical consequence is used that relates to privileges rather than an artificial point system.

Scenario: Brianne asked to use the iPad to play a game during free time. She was told no because the group was about to start a new project. Brianne argued and yelled that she was being treated unfairly because others in the group were allowed to use the iPad. An adult told Brianne to stop arguing and sit in a chair. When she complied, the Corrective Teaching began.

Step 1: Give praise or empathy.

"Brianne, I know how much fun you have playing on the iPad. It's fun for me, too."

[empathy]

Step 2: Describe or demonstrate the inappropriate behavior.

"But let's talk about what just happened. When I told you 'No,' you started to argue and yell at me. That's not acceptable behavior."

Step 3: Issue a negative consequence along with a positive correction statement.

"Because you had such a hard time accepting 'No,' you've earned yourself a chat with me at the start of our next 'free period,' which will shorten your free time [negative consequence]. We're going to talk about how to accept 'No' for an answer. But if you work with me now, we can keep that conversation quick so you'll earn more of your time back [positive correction]. Okay?"

[Brianne nods in agreement.]

Step 4: Describe or demonstrate the appropriate behavior (give the skill steps).

"Great, Brianne. Super job of accepting your consequence [praise]. Now, let's talk about a better way to respond when someone tells you 'No.' Next time, use the skill of 'Accepting "No" for an Answer.' To do this skill, look at the person, say 'okay,' stay calm, and, if you disagree with the answer, come back later to talk about it."

Step 5: Provide a rationale (reason) and request acknowledgement.

"When you can accept a 'No' answer appropriately, you have a much better chance of getting a 'Yes' answer in the future [rationale]. Does that make sense [acknowledgement]?"

Step 6: Practice.

"Okay, let's try practicing the skill. Go ahead and ask me if you can use the iPad, then I'll answer by telling you 'No' because it's time to start a new project. Remember, after I say 'No,' you should look at me, say 'Okay,' and stay calm. Let's give it a shot."

[Brianne practices the skill and follows the steps correctly.]

Step 7: Give feedback, praise, and a positive consequence.

"Awesome job, [praise] Brianne! You were calm and said 'okay' [feedback]. Because you did such a great job following my instructions and practicing the skill steps, our conversation during free period will be quick so you'll have more of your free time back."

Step 8: Offer praise and encouragement.

"Fantastic. I'm really proud of the way you calmed down and worked with me to learn this new skill!"

[The adult fist bumps Brianne.]

Corrective Teaching is a proven method for helping youth learn how to use appropriate behaviors in place of inappropriate behaviors. Three concept areas – description, relationship, and consequence – comprise the Corrective Teaching Interaction. Within these areas are specific steps that provide structure to the teaching process while also allowing adults to develop and strengthen relationships. The effective use of Corrective Teaching can empower kids to make new behaviors a permanent part of their daily lives and enable them to successfully use these behaviors and skills in many different situations.

Promoting Generalization during Teaching

Generalization is addressed in more detail in other sections of this book. (See Chapter 4.) When it comes to specific teaching techniques, it is sufficient to say that several components of Proactive Teaching, Effective Praise, and Corrective Teaching are geared to promote the use of skills across situations. The "rationales" component is probably the most important of these. Well-constructed rationales point out to a youth how learning appropriate styles of interacting with others will produce favorable outcomes in other arenas of their life (including school, with peers, at home, etc.). However, for rationales to be truly effective in getting a youth to learn and implement new skills, the adults working with that youth must know their individual likes and dislikes, values, and experiences very well. Knowledge of what a youth finds important and meaningful in life is critical to fostering the internal motivation to change.

Other specific techniques can be utilized during social skills training in order to increase the potential for generalization and maintenance (Sulzer-Azaroff & Mayer, 1986; Mayer, Sulzer-Azaroff, & Wallace, 2013; Cartledge & Milburn, 1995; Goldstein, Sprafkin, Gershaw, & Klein, 1980; Kurtz, Gaudin, Wodarski, & Howing, 1993). They include:

1. **Teaching in different settings:** This means varying the location of instruction in order to simulate the different situations the youth may encounter. Simultaneously teach the youth to discriminate between situations and successfully identify which skills to use.

2. **Teaching with different people:** This means using more than one caregiver

or staff person to define, model, and role-play the target skills with the youth. It is best if persons who are involved with the youth in other stimulus situations can participate (i.e., the youth's teacher or counselor, a parent, peers, etc.).

3. **"Homework" assignments:** These are commonly used in group social skills training (see Chapter 5) or on an outpatient basis. The youth is given an assignment to use a skill in a particular situation, record the outcome, and report back to the adult who is teaching the skill.

4. **Altering reinforcement contingencies:** This approach increases the natural reinforcement for prosocial behavior. Generalization is enhanced when skills that are taught are ones that parents, teachers, and peers will reinforce more often than the youth's inappropriate responses (Howing, Wodarski, Kurtz, & Gaudin, 1990).

It is apparent that a number of activities within a skill-teaching session with a child can and should be used to promote generalization and maintenance. However, in day-to-day interactions with youth, caregivers should be attuned to the opportunities that are present for rewarding prosocial behaviors and correcting inappropriate behaviors that occur. These two processes themselves are critical to the generalization of skills that are taught in planned, structured teaching situations.

Summary

Teaching children skills and behaviors so they can change for the better is an awesome responsibility. Every situation you face will pose a different, and often difficult, challenge. Having confidence in your abilities and tools – specifically effective teaching methods – and constantly working to improve how you apply them in your service to youth, will be the key to success for you and the young people in your care.

Everyone who shoulders the responsibility of helping, teaching, or caring for children has some ability to teach new skills and appropriate behaviors. Only when a person applies that ability in a compassionate and competent manner, with the best interests of the youth at heart, can the desired results be achieved – a youth who has learned not only how to behave differently but how to live differently.

CHAPTER 4
Generalization of Social Skills

In effective behavior-change programs, youth (or adults) learn and become proficient at using skills and behaviors, and then are able to use them in many situations inside and outside the instructional setting. In other words, a youth is able to apply what they have learned beyond the bounds of the program, with many different people and in many different situations. This is called **generalization,** and it is one of the true measures of the success of social skills training.

Generalization means that skills learned under one set of antecedent (or stimulus) conditions are used under different sets of antecedent (stimulus) conditions. For example, a youth who learns and uses the skill of "Following Instructions" at home with his parents, and then can appropriately use the skill with teachers at school, has learned how to generalize that skill to different situations. Generalization is a skill in and of itself, and it helps youth move from simply performing skills to making cognitive choices about when, where, and how to use them.

Experts, such as Norman Webb (2005), describe the ability to reach a strategic thinking level, moving from describing to explaining to interpreting, as reaching level three in depth of knowledge. Level three activities, such as supporting ideas with details and examples, developing logical arguments, citing evidence, and differentiating between concepts, demonstrate that a youth has moved beyond the ability to recall or relate concepts, but can actually draw conclusions. Generalization of social skills to a variety of settings is a demonstration of this greater depth of knowledge.

Generalization of skills and behaviors is achieved through the process of generalization training. Generalization training is a procedure in which a behavior is reinforced in a number of different stimulus situations until the behavior occurs naturally and reliably across settings. Often, behavior-change programs teach a number of socially important skills and behaviors to clients and then expect them to automatically be able to use the skills and behaviors in new situations. This is often referred to as a "train-and-hope" approach. Successful generalization training, however, employs active methods like practice and role-playing to ensure the learner can successfully use socially important behaviors in a number of relevant social contexts.

Before we examine ways to help youth achieve generalization, a key philosophical point must be made. We must realize that when youth do not or cannot generalize skills and behaviors, it is usually due to the failure of adults, not the youth. Youth seldom choose not to use learned skills in different settings. Adults must assume the responsibility when this happens and must work harder to educate youth in the skill of generalization.

Generalization Training

Gresham, Sugai, and Horner (2001) cite several likely reasons for the lack of generalization in social skills training. One reason is that skills tend to be taught in artificial situations and often are not reinforced in the youth's natural environment. So, one way to achieve generalization is to train those skills or behaviors that are most likely to be reinforced in the natural environment. This approach is called "trapping" and involves developing behavior that falls into the "behavior trap" represented by what happens in the environment when those behaviors are used (Baer & Wolf, 1970). Social skills such as "Maintaining a Conversation," "Accepting Criticism (Feedback) or a Consequence," and "Following Instructions" will probably be socially reinforced by a significant number of people in the youth's environment. The youth is more likely to continue to use these behaviors after the training because natural reinforcers like positive attention and approval by others will reinforce the behaviors.

In terms of the "behavior trap," it is imperative to teach skills that are considered socially valid. The concept of social validity (Wolf, 1978; Carter, 2010) provides a basis for identifying relevant behaviors to be taught. A skill or behavior is socially valid if it is efficient and reliable. An efficient skill produces the expected outcome with less effort and likely some form of reinforcement. A reliable skill produces the expected outcome or reinforcers consistently. If the newly trained skill of "Maintaining a Conversation" leads to increased reinforcement and the desired outcome (peer inclusion), then it is said to be efficient and reliable. Selecting socially valid skills prior to intervention demonstrates how generalization can be programmed into an intervention from the beginning. When possible, parents (or other caregivers) should be involved when determining what social skills would be beneficial to a youth because parents play a critical role in social skill development and generalization (Arthur, Bochner, & Butterfield, 1999).

Promoting Generalization

Now that we have established the necessity of selecting relevant skills to be taught, what is the best way to teach these skills in order to promote generalization?

Whether or not generalization occurs depends heavily on how similar the different stimulus situations are. The more similar these situations are, the more initial generalization there will be between them. Social skills should be taught in situations that are as similar as possible to the environments in which youth can be expected to use the skills. For example, the skill of "Getting the Teacher's Attention" should be taught in situations that closely simulate a classroom setting because that is where a youth ultimately is going to use the skill. Research supports the idea that a new behavior can be taught and learned through direct instructional techniques; many times, however, a skill is taught in a contrived setting and has little meaning or utility to a youth outside of that setting (Gresham, 1998; Gresham, Sugai, & Horner, 2001). This does not mean a skill cannot be discussed and modeled outside the classroom. But to increase the likelihood that the youth will successfully generalize the skill, it is best to actually practice the skill in a classroom or a classroom-like setting.

Such a generalization teaching approach also should include varying the training conditions when possible, training in different locations, using different instructors, and incorporating pairs or small groups of learners to make the training more realistic. When training takes place in an environment that is different from the actual setting, real-life experiences should be used whenever possible and the training should be related to experiences that occur outside the training environment. This means discussing with youth specifically where, when, and with whom skills may be used.

Social skills training also should include some form of "cognitive mediators." Cognitive mediators incorporate a "how-to-think" component into social skills training. They enable youth to assess how well or how poorly they used a skill, and to think about what, if anything, they should do differently the next time they use the skill. Research indicates that cognitive strategies like this can decrease hyperactivity/impulsivity and disruption/aggression, and strengthen prosocial behavior (Robinson, Smith, Miller, & Brownell, 1999).

Caregivers can implement this element by providing clear expectations, imagery, some form of self-talk, such as a rationale for using the skill, and problem-solving strategies. Generalization is enhanced when there is some form of internal motivation to use the skill. For example, a youth who understands that using a particular skill will help her avoid a negative consequence is more likely to use the skill in a variety of settings. The same may be true for a youth who sees that using the skill of "Following Instructions" helps him complete a task faster and earns him a reputation of being trustworthy. The use of cognitive mediators in social skills training should assist the youth in identifying and interpreting social cues, predicting what

may happen next, selecting what skill to use, and evaluating the outcome of using the skill.

To further promote generalization, the final stages of social skills training should involve the use of natural and logical consequences that are very similar to those that will occur in real life. Many programs that teach youth social skills use some form of a motivation system in which youth earn or lose points, tokens, or some other form of consequences, contingent on their behavior. (Boys Town uses a motivation system where youth earn points for appropriate behavior and lose points for inappropriate behavior. When youth have a preset number of points at the end of the day, they can use the points they've earned to purchase privileges and other rewards.)

Ideally, an effective motivation system is paired with praise and other forms of positive attention and approval. This allows caregivers to gradually "fade" a youth off the motivation system and rely on praise, attention, and approval alone to motivate them to continue using positive behavior and skills. For example, as a youth in a program learns the skill of "Following Instructions" and improves her proficiency with it, she receives points or tokens for using the skill in applicable situations. The program staff then gradually fades the use of points and increases social praise for the youth's use of the skill. Eventually, the youth will be motivated to continue to use the skill by praise and other forms of approval, the natural and logical consequences she would receive for appropriate behavior at home or school.

The key to any successful social skills training program is what happens when a youth demonstrates a skill spontaneously. When this occurs in a new setting, reinforcement of the behavior should be increased enough to ensure the youth will consistently maintain the behavior. If a youth fails to use a skill or uses the skill inappropriately, there should be a consistent method of correction, with emphasis on teaching the alternative behavior.

Summary

In a manner of speaking, generalization is the pot of gold at the end of the social skills training rainbow. When a youth shows that they can competently and correctly generalize a skill to a variety of situations, it is a sign of success that the youth has moved to a new level of skill competency.

Generalization is most likely to be achieved when social skills training and practice occur in situations that are as similar as possible to the situations where a youth will be expected to use new skills. Regardless of where youth are learning skills – in a child-service program, at school, in a youth shelter, in a clinical setting, at home – the ultimate goal is to equip youth for social interactions by giving them the skills they need and to prepare them to use those skills in many situations. Social skills training without generalization only provides youth with a list of behaviors that lead to appropriate behavior. Knowing how and when to apply those behaviors is the real key to long-lasting and meaningful change that, in the end, helps kids overcome problems and be successful.

CHAPTER 5
Teaching Skills in Group Settings

An alternative way to teach interpersonal skills to children and adolescents is to use a group-teaching format. Bandura (1989) stated that most social learning takes place by observing others and the results of their actions. A group setting provides an immediate social environment in which specific skills can be taught and practiced, and in which a youth can gradually become sensitized to their role as a group member. This is an important process because of the numerous "groups" all youth must function in as a part of normal family and community life (school classes, peer groups, sports teams, work groups, etc.).

By incorporating social skills group training into a setting where a child is receiving intervention, education, or other types of care, adults can address individual goals and target areas and effectively teach and maintain skills. In other words, the advantages of a group-teaching format can be applied to each youngster's individual benefit. In this chapter, we review these advantages, some previous uses of group skills training, a structured format for conducting skills groups, and techniques for maintaining productive group meetings.

Advantages of Group Teaching

There are many reasons for incorporating skill-building groups into child care programs and educational settings as a way to augment individual efforts. The group provides a ready-made social setting in which to assess each member's ongoing social functioning under a variety of circumstances, as well as a more natural teaching situation (Trower, Bryant, & Argyle, 2015). The youth's ability to participate in group activities, concentrate on lessons and tasks, and respond to performance demands may give adults valuable insight into potential problems in other situations that would require similar skills (such as being in a classroom).

Because skills-training groups allow several youth to participate together, there is increased opportunity for each member to share their responses and differing perspectives to problem situations, and to perhaps generate alternative ways of handling difficult circumstances (Hazel, Schumaker, Sherman, & Sheldon-Wildgen, 1983; Vernon, Hazel, & Schumaker, 1988). This may be especially important for those children with learning or cognitive deficits who tend to rigidly stick to one set of responses in diverse situations. Participation in a group may let children know that there are numerous ways to handle stressful or demanding situations and that their previous strategies represent only one option. Many times, a child's peers will communicate this message most effectively. Several studies with autistic children reveal that involving peers in social skills interventions provides children with autism the opportunity to observe, imitate, and learn from the social behaviors of their typically developing peers (Kamps et al., 2002).

There also is evidence that behaviors and skills learned in a group setting may come under control of a greater number of clearly different stimuli, thus increasing the probability that learned skills will be used in situations outside the group (Howing, Wodarski, Kurtz, & Gaudin, 1990; Kurtz, Gaudin, Wodarski, & Howing, 1993). The result, therefore, would be greater generalization of the specific skills taught in the group to diverse situations that youth face and greater maintenance of these skills following intervention. This is especially true when several different training techniques (as well as different adult trainers) are used to enhance and prompt generalization.

ADVANTAGES OF GROUP SETTINGS

1. Assessment of social functioning in the group

2. Training in more realistic settings

3. Opportunity to share experiences and options

4. Enhanced generalization and maintenance of skills

5. Cost efficient and time efficient

Figure 1

In addition to these benefits, providing skills training in group settings can increase the number of youth who may be served by a particular program or service, or may increase the cost-effectiveness of

a program with limited staff or resources. The advantages of conducting skills training in group settings are summarized in Figure 1.

Group skills training has been used in many treatment settings, schools, and outpatient programs. The populations and age groups that have been served using this format have been extremely varied as well.

One group of youth that has received particular attention in regard to skills training is juvenile delinquents. This is no doubt due to the well-documented relationship between low social skill functioning and delinquent behavior in adolescents and young adults. Several studies have shown the effectiveness of using group teaching techniques with groups of juvenile delinquents. In one report (Shivrattan, 1988), incarcerated male delinquents participated in a social skills training program designed to increase cognitive empathy in participants. The results showed that these youth improved on measures of being considerate, insight, and anger control. In addition, a one-year follow-up of the participants revealed that they had lower rates of recidivism and better community adjustment than their counterparts in a control group.

Skills groups also have been conducted with court-adjudicated adolescents on an outpatient basis (Hazel et al., 1983). This typically involves having youth attend a weekly group meeting that lasts 1½ to 2 hours and focuses on a limited number of target skills (e.g., "Following Instructions," "Accepting Criticism (Feedback) or a Consequence," and "Resisting Peer Pressure"). In an evaluation of one such program for court-adjudicated youth, Hazel et al. (1983) demonstrated that this effort also produced lower rates of recidivism for group participants after one year than were evident in a comparison group that did not participate in the training.

Skills-training groups have been used as part of inpatient psychiatric and day-treatment programs for adolescents as well. For example, when conversation skills were taught to inpatient children and adolescents, the result was better communication behaviors demonstrated both with peers and with unfamiliar adults (Hansen, St. Lawrence, & Christoff, 1989). The effects of an improved style of communication can enhance the other therapeutic gains made by each youth within the psychiatric setting.

This also has been considered true for social skills groups conducted as part of day-treatment programming for emotionally disturbed adolescents (Friedman, Quick, Mayo, & Palmer, 1983). In this case, the training resulted in better peer relationships and better conflict resolution within the program, and thus greater gains by the program's participants overall.

Skills intervention based on a group format has been used effectively in educational settings with both disabled and non-disabled youngsters. In-school social skill instruction has been used with disruptive students of all ages in urban and rural high schools to reduce antisocial behavior and discipline referrals. An additional benefit of this approach is a corresponding increase in on-task behavior from students and better performance on curriculum measures. The implication here is that school may, in fact, be the ideal place in which to conduct social skills training groups because the positive effects of training may be more pronounced there anyway.

According to the National Research Council (2012), succeeding in "work and life… is associated with cognitive, intrapersonal and interpersonal competencies that allow individuals to adapt effectively

to changing situations" (p. 70). The Council recommends developing valid and reliable measurements of 21st century skills (self-management, critical thinking, collaboration, and problem solving, among others) and incorporating the development of those skills in core academic subject areas.

Experts in positive behavioral intervention and support (PBIS, sometimes abbreviated as SWPBIS when referring to a school-wide implementation) have studied the positive effects of social skills teaching on students from early education through secondary school. Universal interventions and secondary interventions have shown positive results on students' skill development and behavioral change. These results support the use of skill groups/small-group instruction for the development of prosocial skills, and suggest a positive connection between academic success and prosocial behavior in class (Gresham, Sugai, & Horner, 2001; Lane, Wehby, Menzies, Doukas, Munton, & Gregg, 2003; Moote, Smyth, & Wodarski, 1999; Powers, 2003).

For many young people, school remains the biggest challenge in their lives. Gresham (1995) notes that schools are one of the most important settings in which children acquire, develop, and refine the skills that are essential for establishing and maintaining interpersonal relationships. By learning new sets of positive, prosocial behaviors within the school environment, students may be more immediately equipped to deal with academic and social obstacles.

Structure and Format of the Skills Group

In deciding on the structure, scheduling, and content of a skills-training group, a large number of factors must be considered. These include the size and makeup of the group, characteristics of the participants, and decisions regarding who will lead the training exercises. The content of any given session may vary according to the age, developmental level, abilities, and presenting problems of the youth.

Despite the flexibility possible in designing and implementing a skills-training program, a few generalities can be made based on previous experience. For example, small groups of 10 or fewer youth are thought to be more effective with regular instruction occurring at least twice a week (Howing et al., 1990). Using more than one trainer, preferably a male and a female, also is recommended in order to enhance the potential for generalization and to help monitor the behavior of the participants.

The youths' previous grouping or participation in groups in other primary intervention programs most often determines those youths' characteristics. For example, a social skills group may include all of the children in a particular hospital unit or special education class. In these cases, the group members may already know each other or have formed some friendships. On the other hand, group members may be drawn from the population of young people adjudicated by a county juvenile court for a one-month period. In this case, special activities would be necessary at the outset to introduce group members and make each comfortable with the situation. In both of these examples, however, a positive group atmosphere needs to be created at the outset and maintained by the group leaders.

Ang and Hughes (2001) found that skills-training intervention delivered in the context of groups of only antisocial peers produced smaller benefits than did skills-training interventions that avoided group-ing only antisocial peers together. This is critical since the issues under discussion may include alternatives to delinquency or drug behavior, which group members should not glamorize or brag about. (Techniques for maintaining a productive training environment are covered later in this chapter.)

Issues related to grouping and participant characteristics also include whether to combine groups of children who are different in their functioning level and/or handicap. It is appropriate to combine higher-functioning and lower-functioning children in a social skills training group as long as the behaviors of the higher-functioning children are generally attainable and capable of being modeled and performed by the lower-functioning members (Howing et al., 1990). In fact, the inclusion of nondisabled peers into a social skills group for disabled children is quite positive because the nondisabled children's behaviors are more likely to be modeled and imitated, especially if these behaviors result in peer reinforcement (Gresham, 1981; Gresham, Van, & Cook, 2006).

Prior to beginning a skills-training group, trainers should invest a good deal of time in preparation and planning. The setting should be arranged, materials organized, and reinforcers planned in advance in order to reward positive performance and participation. Additional guidelines for specifically planning instructional content include (Oden, 1980):

1. **Select content focus.** Select the one or two skills that will be covered in that particular session.

2. **Organize the content.** The content and materials should be clearly organized, with particular emphasis on matching the language to be used to the ages and

---

GROUP TEACHING COMPONENTS

1. Start the group session.

2. Introduce the topic or skill.

3. Define and model the skill.

4. Role-play the target skill.

5. Have youth earn positive consequences (Individual/Group).

6. Give a generalization assignment and prompt.

Figure 2

developmental levels of the participants.

3. **Prepare the oral presentation of material.** Plan examples to be used and role-play scenes that can be acted out. Prepare answers to different responses from group members and an explanation of how inappropriate behavior will be addressed.

4. **Select activities for peer interaction and reinforcement.** The skills instruction may be built around normal activities or a special game. The trainer also should plan reinforcing activities for group members at the conclusion of the session.

Group Teaching Format

The specific components and format of skills training are summarized in Figure 2. A definition of each component and an example of what the component might sound like in a residential program follows. (For ease of presentation, only one leader

is conducting the session in the example. Usually, it is best to have two co-leaders; other staff members can assist, depending on the size of the group and the activities that are planned.) While a residential program is used in this example, it is important to remember that group training can be used in a variety of settings with a variety of children.

1. **Start the group session:** The group leader brings the session to order with a clear beginning prompt or cue that is used consistently to start each session. The leader then welcomes the participants and reviews the group rules and the behaviors expected from group members. (See Figure 3 on page 57.) The group could then review the previous lesson or any assignments that were given at the end of the previous lesson. The leader should also remind group members about the reinforcers or rewards available for positive group participation or skill performance.

Example:

Leader: *"Okay, guys, let's bring this meeting to order. [pause] Good, thanks for quieting down. Before we get started, let's review the rules we established for our group meetings. Chase, can you tell us one?"*

Chase: *"Yeah, we raise our hands before talking and don't just call out."*

Leader: *"Good, Chase, that's right! Raising our hands will help our meetings be more organized and probably go faster. Does anyone else have a rule they would like to give? If not, then let's see if you have your homework from our last session. Please pass it up front and remember that if you are turning in your assignment, you can earn an extra 15 minutes of game time on the computer. Also, I want to remind you* *guys that if you work hard on today's skills, you can earn up to a half hour of extra TV time this afternoon. Okay, let's get started."*

2. **Introduce the topic or skill:** Here the group leader introduces the skill or skills that will be the focus of the session. They are stated as a concept and labeled by the name that everyone will consistently call them. Then, the leader talks about situations where the target skill may be used. The leader may give an example of these situations first, then ask for suggestions from the group. This not only promotes more meaningful involvement, but also helps to reinforce the ongoing level of understanding of the group members. The leader also may ask the youth how they have handled these types of situations in the past and whether those responses have resulted in negative consequences.

Example:

Leader: *"We are going to talk today about a skill that will really help you all here in the program and when you go home to your parents. The skill is 'Accepting "No" for an Answer.' This skill has to do with what you might say and do when you want to do something and the person you ask tells you 'No.' For example, if you wanted to go to a party, you might ask your mom if it's all right to do that. But your mom might say that there might be drinking or drugs there, so the answer is 'No.' What are some other times when someone might tell you 'No?'"*

Brooklyn: *"I might ask my teacher if I can get a drink, and he could tell me 'No.'"*

Leader: *"That's a good example, Brooklyn. Tell me what you have done when things like*

that have happened before?"

Brooklyn: *"I guess I usually got pretty mad and went and got a drink anyway."*

Leader: *"Okay, and can anybody tell us what could happen if you get mad, lose your temper in school, and get sent out of class?"*

Alicia: *"I know when I've gotten mad like that I usually ended up in the office."*

Leader: *"You're right. That could happen. So today we are going to talk about a different way to handle getting a 'No' answer."*

3. **Define and model the skill:** The leader now verbally and visually defines the component behaviors of the target skill. This is first done with a verbal explanation of each step of the skill. During this time, the leader lists any youth responses on chart paper or a whiteboard. The leader then models these behaviors by using a situation based on one of the examples given during the previous step. Modeling a situation can be repeated or several situations can be acted out in order to help the youth understand. The group leader also explains a reason for using the appropriate responses rather than inappropriate ones that may result in negative consequences for the youth. The leader then asks the group members for more examples.

Example:

Leader*: "Whenever you receive a 'No' answer, here's what you should do. First, continue looking at the person you are talking to. Second, acknowledge the answer by saying something like 'Okay' or 'Sure, no problem' in a pleasant tone of voice. Third, don't use any behaviors like whining, arguing, or mumbling under your* breath. And fourth, if you have a question, ask the person if you can discuss your request later on. If you do those things, you will be accepting a 'No' answer really well. In fact, to show you guys what we're talking about, Alicia and I will practice this skill using Brooklyn's example of asking his teacher if he can get a drink during class."

[The leader and Alicia model the skill.]

Leader: "Did everyone see what we did here? When I told Alicia 'No' about getting a drink, she continued looking at me, said 'Okay, maybe later,' and did not argue or whine. The reason it is so important to use these behaviors is that the person who told you 'No' this time may be willing to negotiate later on for something else if you can accept the first answer without arguing or becoming aggressive. Does everybody understand that? Can anyone else think of another reason to accept 'No' answers appropriately? What about an example of what might happen in the situation where the youth asks to go to the party?"

Ty: "If you go to the party anyway, you could get an MIP [minor in possession] and could end up in more trouble."

Leader: "That's right, Ty. Sometimes we get a 'No' answer to protect us from potentially bad experiences. If you ignore the answer and go to the party anyway, you may find yourself in bigger trouble with greater consequences."

4. **Role-play the target skill:** In this step, each youth is given an opportunity to rehearse the behaviors of the target skill several times in order to learn and begin to generalize the component behaviors. This begins with the leader reviewing the components of the skill and then setting up realistic role-play situations, possibly based on earlier examples offered by the youth. Each

youth should first practice the skill with the leader, and then with a peer. The leader follows up each practice with immediate behavioral feedback for the youth by praising the youth's efforts, describing the parts of the role-play that were correctly done to criteria, and describing any component behaviors that were left out or not performed to criteria.

While it is important that effective teaching takes place, the emphasis also should be on making the practices fun and reinforcing, and avoiding a test-like atmosphere. The leader (or other staff members) should closely monitor each role-play and provide feedback to youth on their level of participation and seriousness. The leader should end the role-plays by praising the youth for their efforts and having a discussion about what was practiced.

Example:

Leader: "Okay, then, let's review the steps of accepting 'No' for an answer one more time. Then we can practice it together. Whenever someone tells you 'No,' you should keep looking at the person, acknowledge the answer in a calm voice, and not argue or pout. And if you disagree or have a question, bring it up later. Chase, how about you practicing once with me? In this situation, Chase, I'll play the part of your dad and you're going to ask me if you can go out with some friends. When I tell you 'No,' I want you to use all of the behaviors we just described. After we practice, you and Alicia can try a few situations together."

[The leader and Chase role-play the situation.]

Leader: "Chase, that was great! You kept looking at me the whole time we were talking, said

'Okay, maybe I can hang out with friends at another time and place,' and did not argue or start whining. That's just how to accept 'No' for an answer. Why don't you and Alicia try it? In your situation, Chase can be Alicia's boss, and Alicia can play an employee who is asking to leave work early."

[Chase and Alicia role-play the situation.]

Leader: *"You both did a really super job on this skill. You stayed on task and listened really well. I hope you see how accepting 'No' answers in an appropriate way can help you out in school, on a summer job, and back home with your parents."*

5. **Have youth earn positive consequences (Individual/Group):** At this point, each group member earns a consequence for the amount and quality of their participation in the group. The positive consequences that are awarded can be either privilege-based or token-based, or a combination that incorporates the motivation system that is in effect in the program. At the conclusion of the session, a reward, such as a special snack or activity, can be offered to the entire group based on some pre-arranged contingency agreement. The important aspects of the positive consequence component are that the rewards are meaningful and valued by the participants, and are specifically paired with whatever behavior the leader wishes to see again in the future and considers a priority (i.e., participation and effort versus flawless skill performance).

   NOTE: If the leader wants to teach a second skill, they can either save the positive consequences until all the practices and role-plays are completed

or provide a consequence after each skill is practiced individually.

Example:

Leader: *"Each of you did really well today. Brooklyn and Alicia, you've each earned 500 points for practicing accepting 'No' for an answer and 500 points for listening and participating in our group today. Chase, since accepting 'No' is a special target area for you, you've earned 1,000 points for doing so well at the role-play and 500 points for staying on task in our group. Everyone also worked so hard today that we are going down the street to get some ice cream when we are done here. And when we get back, you all can play video games for 15 minutes."*

6. **Give a generalization assignment and prompt:** In the final component of the group-training format, the leader may give an assignment that the youth are to complete outside the group and report on at the next session. The generalization assignment is a key ingredient in helping the youth learn to use skills in many different situations (Goldstein et al., 1980). The assignments themselves can range from written homework reviews of group topics to journal recordings on the success (or lack thereof) encountered in implementing the target skills. The group is then adjourned with more prompts and encouragement for group members, and an opportunity to use privileges or rewards.

Example:

Leader: *"Your assignment for our next meeting is to record in your notebooks all the times people tell you 'No' this week and what your response is to them. And if you can, write down*

**POSITIVE AND NEGATIVE
GROUP BEHAVIORS TO ADDRESS**

Behaviors to reinforce

1. Raising hands and waiting to be called on

2. Being attentive and remaining on task

3. Volunteering and participating in activities

4. Making positive comments about others

5. Following directions and accepting feedback

Behaviors to correct

1. Calling out or leaving seat without permission

2. Distracting others, fidgeting, or yawning

3. Making negative comments or insulting others

4. Bragging about inappropriate behavior

5. Arguing, noncompliance, and complaining

Figure 3

what their reaction is when you accept 'No' in a positive way by looking at them, saying 'Okay,' and not arguing. I'll be interested to see how this skill, and all of the skills we talk about here, help you in situations that have caused you problems in the past. If there isn't anything else, we'll adjourn our meeting and

go down the street for that ice cream! Thanks, everybody."

This sample format for a skills-training group is limited only by the creativity of the leader (and other participating adults) and the needs of the youth in the group. Variations in terms of role-play activities, audio-visuals, reinforcers, etc., only serve to enrich the process and make it more enjoyable for the youth. Leaders of social skills groups have ranked boredom and inattentiveness as the primary barriers to their groups' smooth functioning (Howing et al., 1990). Boredom can be addressed by varying teaching methods and materials, as well as the reinforcement available, in order to maintain the youths' interest and enthusiasm.

Inattentiveness is one of many ongoing behaviors that should be closely monitored during the group session and corrected if necessary. Some techniques for addressing the behavior of group participants are explained next.

Maintaining a Productive Group Atmosphere

A number of procedures can be used to help maintain a group environment that is enjoyable, yet productive and goal-directed. This is possible only if group members display certain behaviors while participating that are not distracting, disruptive, or apathetic (nonparticipation). However, given that youth usually are referred to a group due to lower-than-expected social skill functioning, group leaders and other involved adults must assume that the positive behaviors necessary for a smooth-running group will occur only with a significant amount of proactive and ongoing teaching. The main purpose of this teaching is to educate group members and prevent disruptive and other inappropriate behaviors during group sessions. Even then, it is quite likely that some youth will become distracted or irritable, or even completely lose emotional control during a group session. Overall, the best approach to use is one that has been thought out and even rehearsed in advance of these problems. That's why it is necessary for group leaders to define which behaviors will be praised, which will be addressed through Corrective Teaching, and what interventions will occur if a youth must be removed from the group. Consequences for positive and negative behaviors should be planned out in advance as well.

Once group leaders have created a list of expected behaviors (rules and guidelines) and corresponding consequences for group sessions, they can teach these behaviors to each potential group member individually before they meet for the first time. They then can review the behaviors at the group's first session. After that, each meeting can begin with a brief review of the group's rules as a preventive prompt and a reminder to each member of their responsibility. Visual prompts such as posters, handouts, and note cards also can serve as effective cues for using appropriate skills. This preventive work is rounded off by reviewing the rewards that are available at the conclusion of the group session for individuals who display attentive behaviors and participate in activities.

The adults who are leading a skills group must closely monitor the youths' behaviors during the group session. As we mentioned earlier, it is a good idea to have two co-leaders for each session. Should a youth require individual attention or corrective feedback, one leader can continue with the group while the other works with that youth. The leaders should remember, however, that ongoing praise and reinforcement of positive group behaviors is as equally critical as corrective feedback for negative behaviors. Praise and reinforcement not only help ensure that youth will continue to use positive behaviors, but also enhance the positive atmosphere within the group. Figure 3 features a partial list of behaviors that should be addressed in a group setting.

In addition to the leaders' ongoing prompting and teaching to youth behaviors, numerous other approaches can be used to maintain productive skills groups with children and adolescents. One technique for intervening in serious peer conflicts is called "fair fighting" (Friedman et al., 1983). In this technique, when two youth become extremely angry at each other, they are initially separated and each one goes to a private area to talk to an adult alone. Each youth tells their side of the argument to the adult, who gives the youth instructions to calm down. The youth and the two adults then get together, and the youth observe the adults discuss the problem issue from the youths' perspective and arrive at a resolution. This serves to defuse the immediate crisis situation and allows adults to model appropriate conflict resolution strategies for the youth.

Summary

Teaching skills in group settings can be a viable alternative for many children and youth who require instruction in interpersonal skills. The group setting functions almost like a "sheltered workshop" for socially deficient youth where they can learn, practice, and generalize skills that will be critical to their success in almost every arena of life. Group teaching also can function effectively as an additional intervention for each youth individually. A youth's specific needs are best addressed through a comprehensive, integrated approach that prepares the youth for less-restrictive living or educational alternatives, and improves their overall social functioning.

One hallmark of the Boys Town Model® is a system called "Self-Government," which is designed to encourage group participation and decision-making. One component of the Self-Government System is a nightly meeting of the youth and their caregivers called "Family Meeting." Within the structure of this meeting, each youth has an opportunity to discuss problems, offer potential solutions, and even vote on certain house rules. The caregivers use this nightly meeting to encourage group problem-solving, give each youth a chance to provide input about the operation of the program, and teach a wide variety of important social skills (discussion skills, giving and receiving feedback, reporting problems, etc.). In this way, each youth's individual Service Plan is augmented by what is taught and reinforced during Family Meeting.

CHAPTER 6
Social Skills and Service Planning

Children and adolescents, like all human beings, are part of social groups. They depend on relationships with others to meet even their most basic needs. A child's sense of well-being is directly related to their success, or lack of success, in dealing with significant others.

Early in life, young people learn that there are consequences, both positive and negative, attached to how they interact with others and how they choose to respond in social situations. This process of "socialization" begins in the earliest interactions between infant and parent; it prepares kids for more difficult situations later in childhood and through the teenage years. Ideally, lessons learned at each stage in a child's development become the tools they use to successfully meet the challenges presented at later stages of life.

Today, young people face an increasingly complicated world. Many factors can affect a child's ability to learn new skills and change behaviors. Age, developmental level, family problems, substance abuse, economic pressures, the lure of gangs, delinquency, and many other external issues threaten children physically, emotionally, and spiritually. Also, internal issues like possible chemical imbalances in a child's brain, genetic traits inherited from a child's parents, medical problems, and others can have an impact on learning and behavior. In addition, a child's thoughts and feelings – the way a child looks at the world – have been shaped by their past experiences and play a major role in how a young person interacts with others.

During the past few decades, a convincing body of evidence indicates that unless children achieve minimal social competence by about age 6, they have a high probability of being at risk into adulthood in several ways (Ladd, 2000; Parker & Asher, 1987). Other research (Hartup & Moore, 1990; Kinsey, 2000; Ladd & Profilet, 1996; McClellan & Kinsey, 1997; Parker & Asher, 1987; Rogoff, 1990) suggests that a child's long-term social and emotional adaptation, academic and cognitive development, and citizenship are enhanced by frequent opportunities to strengthen social competence during childhood. All of these factors must be considered when developing effective intervention for youth.

In order to successfully cope with these external and internal issues, young people must learn how to interact with others in socially acceptable ways and make appropriate decisions in social situations. In treatment settings, this means developing an individual service plan for each youth that identifies the youth's needs, strengths, and deficiencies, and incorporates social skill instruction (along with other interventions) to address these areas. This chapter focuses on the reasons children need intervention and the role of teaching social skills in service planning.

Why Kids Misbehave

Youth require intervention for many reasons. At Boys Town, we have determined that one of the most influential factors in the development of behavioral and/ or mental health problems is that youth have not yet learned the social skills needed to overcome the problems in their lives. In most cases, when troubled youth require intervention, the environments they come from have significantly contributed to and fostered the formation of problem behaviors and/or mental health difficulties

A number of factors contained within the home, community, and school are related to antisocial behavior (Mayer, 2001). However, a factor that cuts across all three of these areas is an aversive or punitive environment (DeBaryshe, Patterson, & Capaldi, 1993; Dishion, 1992; Elliott, 1992; Mayer, 1995). Research has shown us that aversive or punitive environments predictably promote antisocial behaviors such as aggression, violence, vandalism, and escape (Berkowitz, 1983; Mayer, 1995). However, these learned inappropriate behaviors and skills serve a purpose: They enable the youth to get what they need and want.

Over time, these same behaviors and skills become reinforced and strengthened, and eventually spill over to other environments (e.g., classrooms, sports teams, jobs, relationships with peers and adults, and so on). In these new settings, youth try to use the same negative behaviors that were "successful" for them in the past. But when they don't work, kids flounder, not knowing what it takes to be successful. So, in order for youth to succeed in familiar and new environments, situations, and relationships, they must learn new prosocial skills that will help them get their needs met in ways that are more socially acceptable.

With social skill instruction, youth learn skills that are determined to be the most functional for them and will produce the best long-term results. This means that every youth requires individual intervention. Some youngsters will initially need to learn the most basic skills (e.g., "Following Instructions," "Accepting Consequences," "Accepting 'No' for an Answer," etc.) so that a foundation can be laid for learning more complex skills (e.g., "Expressing Feelings Appropriately," "Resisting Peer Pressure," "Using Spontaneous Problem-Solving," etc.). Many times, caregivers and other adults will need to gradually shape a youth's behavior by patiently teaching basic social skills so that the youth can learn the final desired behavior. This can be a slow, arduous process for caregivers and youth, but it is necessary if the youth is to overcome their problems.

The use of appropriate social skills involves an immensely complex chain of rapidly occurring interpersonal events. For youth, especially those suffering from behavioral and mental health disorders that dramatically limit their emotional and cognitive functioning, correctly performing these skills at the right time can be an overwhelming task. They have considerable difficulty organizing and blending their behaviors into smooth-flowing interactions with others, particularly under stressful conditions. So, supervisors in intervention or care settings should encourage caregivers to adjust their teaching techniques, vocabulary, and interpersonal behaviors to best meet the learning style of each youth.

When assigning social skills for intervention, it is important for a caregiver or team (i.e., supervisors, caregivers, and other adults involved with the youth) to take into account individual factors like the age and developmental level of the youth, the severity of the youth's behaviors, the length of time a youth has been exposed to social skill instruction, and so on. These factors play a pivotal role in the success or failure of each youth's service plan. Once the most appropriate skills have been identified and prioritized, caregivers can use various teaching interactions to reinforce and teach youth new prosocial ways of getting their needs met. (At Boys Town, these interactions include Proactive Teaching, Effective Praise, and Corrective Teaching. See Chapter 3.) It also is critical to identify and target the specific situations and antecedent conditions in which the problem behavior occurs. (See Chapter 2.)

Culture and background also greatly influence behaviors, appearance, expression of affect or feelings, thoughts and cognitions, and language. Because all behavior is culture-based, social behaviors need to be defined and interpreted in a cultural context. Culture is not inherited but learned, passed on over generations and transmitted largely through the institutions of family and school. Parenting practices and family dynamics greatly influence a child's beliefs, values, social attitudes, and eventual behavioral patterns that are reflective of these teachings (Cartledge & Milburn, 1996).

As we've noted, one part of successful service planning is to identify and target appropriate social skills. Thus, a team must consider a child's culture and the critical role it plays in their behaviors, thoughts, and perceptions. For example, looking at an adult is the first step in almost all of the social skills that kids are taught at Boys Town. However, this behavior may be a sign of disrespect or defiance for children in some cultures. Knowing that a child of a specific culture holds such a belief directly affects how one teaches social skills to that child. Skill steps may have to be modified to meet the child's needs, and the child may have to learn to determine whether or not to use all of the steps of a skill in different situations.

Service Planning for Youth Problems and Behaviors

The appropriate choice of skills to teach youth is critical to the teaching process and the eventual success of the learner. This is true for all youth behaviors, but it's especially true when a caregiver or team is confronted with particularly difficult or troublesome behaviors from their youth. Boys Town's working definition of "difficult" youth problems includes those behaviors that can cause harm to the youth and others, that persist chronically over time, and that may eventually lead to negative program departure and other negative consequences for the youth. This definition includes behaviors such as stealing, physical aggression, chronic noncompliance, running away, truancy, sexual acting out and sexual aggression, and drug use – all of which necessitate a systematic approach to service planning and target skill selection.

In general terms, the team decides what skills to target for "typical" youth problems or intervention by first analyzing the functional relationships that exist in the youth's environment that appear to reinforce the problem behaviors. It also is critical that the specific situations and antecedent conditions in which the behaviors occur be identified and targeted. Caregivers then can begin preventive measures through Proactive Teaching and system-

---

SERVICE PLANNING PROCESS

1. Problem inventory

2. Problem selection

3. Problem specification

4. Baselining

5. Specification of service goals

6. Formulation of intervention strategies

7. Follow-up/Revision

8. Maintenance

Figure 1

atically begin to teach appropriate alternative response sets (i.e., the individual skills listed in the Social Skills Curriculum). The team must be sure, however, that the targeted skills directly address the problem behavior and occur under the same situational variables that are associated with the problem behavior being treated.

Oftentimes, a youth may have many negative behaviors and skill deficits, or have particularly serious behavior problems. In the area of identifying which social skills to teach and how to teach them, a systematic analysis of a youth's problem behaviors and the contingencies that appear to be supporting them is necessary when developing or revising a service plan. A process used at Boys Town for formulating a "specialized" Service Plan for difficult youth problems is summarized in Figure 1. An explanation of each step in the process

follows. This process can be adapted by programs that develop or wish to develop service plans for their youth.

1. **Problem inventory.** The team begins by generating a list of all relevant problem behaviors the youth is displaying. This is a brainstorming session designed to inventory all of the youth's behavioral deficits currently being observed by team members (i.e., caregivers, teachers at school, coaches, program supervisors, therapists, parents, etc.). The problem behaviors need not be listed in any particular order or priority, but as they are mentioned by team members who are involved directly with the youth. The process of prioritization begins later. This step also gives caregivers a chance to discuss any frustrations they are having in working with the youth and to deal with any negative emotions they may be experiencing.

2. **Problem selection.** In this step, the team begins to discuss and then decide what behaviors listed in the youth's problem inventory appear to be of the greatest immediate concern. Supervisors or therapists (or whoever takes the lead) assist this decision-making process by prompting discussion on issues such as: 1) What problem behavior occurs most often?; 2) What behavior relates most closely to several other behaviors that were listed?; 3) What behavior causes the most trouble or failure for the youth?; 4) What behavior presents the greatest danger to others?; and 5) What behavior causes the most distress to the adults, family members, or peers who interact with the youth? In this step, the team should prioritize the problem behaviors that were gener-

ated and select the primary behavioral issues to be addressed first. The final choice of what problem behaviors to focus on should also be left to the primary caregiver or those who work closely with the youth. Problems can be made worse when team members differ widely on what behaviors are the most disruptive or difficult to address. Behaviors can be treated most effectively when all team members consistently respond to targeted problem behaviors in a well-defined manner.

3. **Problem specification.** In this step, the problem behaviors the team has chosen to address are clearly defined and specified. This is necessary in order to facilitate more effective intervention by the primary caregivers and quicker learning of alternative behaviors by the youth. First, the actual circumstances in which the problem behaviors consistently occur are noted, as well as other variables such as time of day, location, and people who usually are present when the behaviors occur. It also is important to note the social or verbal interactions (antecedents) that take place immediately before the youth engages in the inappropriate behaviors. These factors help determine the social skill areas in which teaching will take place with the youth.

In addition, the team specifies the youth's actual verbal and physical problem behaviors. Whether the youth's voice becomes elevated or sullen, or whether their verbal statements are sarcastic or threatening are important in defining appropriate responses. When problem behaviors are clearly defined, the team is able to more easily identify the appropriate alternative re-

sponses to teach. In addition to specifying the youth's problem behaviors, the team should list the typical consequences that have followed the inappropriate behavior. This would include the consequences (e.g., restricting privileges, tokens/points, chores, etc.) that caregivers have used in the past when trying to treat the problem, as well as the social responses of others (e.g., attention, ignoring, getting upset) who have been present when the youth displayed the inappropriate behaviors. This analysis can increase the team's insights into what contingencies have been supporting the youth's problematic responses.

The problem specification step ends when the team has identified the alternative skills – or "target skills" – to teach the youth in the same situations or circumstances that the problem behaviors previously occurred. The target skills should be "functional" in that they empower the youth to appropriately handle the situations that have caused the most problems. The emphasis should be on choosing skills that eventually will be reinforcing to the youth and help them meet service goals and needs in a socially acceptable manner.

4. **Baselining.** It is critical for the team to have some knowledge of how often a youth's target behaviors occur. By recording these behaviors daily, weekly, or monthly, caregivers can measure the effectiveness of their teaching over time. A "baseline" measurement is the frequency of a particular behavior's occurrence prior to introducing a new intervention. This measurement can be obtained in formal and informal

ways (e.g., charting, frequency count, estimating, data collection, moving a penny from one pocket to the other when behavior occurs, etc.). The team can derive a formal baseline measurement from systematic observation of the youth in various circumstances, and from carefully recorded clinical/intervention documentation.

An informal baseline measurement can be based on the caregivers' recall of when, where, how often, and under what circumstances a behavior occurs. The goal is to obtain the most accurate measure possible to use as a comparison after the teaching strategy has been in place for a period of time. The team also should estimate how often the youth may use the appropriate replacement skill. This will help the team evaluate whether the caregivers' teaching is increasing the youth's use of the skill while decreasing the negative behavior that was targeted.

5. **Specification of service goals.** At this point in the service planning process for social skill instruction, the team must decide, given the current level of the youth's functioning, what percent of the time they would initially like to see the youth use the target skill. For example, the baselining step reveals that a particular youth correctly follows the caregivers' instructions only two out of every 10 times and refuses to follow instructions the other eight times. Caregivers might then plan to teach the skill of "Following Instructions" to the youth for the first two weeks of intervention with the goal of having him improve to five out of 10 times. Eventually, the goal should be increased to 90 percent, or even 100

percent. Remember, however, that it is important for both the youth and the team that initial skill goals are reasonable and obtainable.

Goal specification also should be related to the components of the particular skill being taught. For example, the eventual goal of teaching a youth to follow instructions would be to have the youth use all of the skill's component behaviors (i.e., look at the person, say "Okay," do the task, and check back) when directed to engage in an activity by caregivers, teachers at school, parents, and others. By specifying the behaviors to be used in "instruction" situations, caregivers are more likely to be consistent in their expectations and teaching, which enables the youth to be more successful in meeting those expectations and being rewarded for doing so.

6. **Formulation of intervention strategies.** In this step, the team agrees on what strategies will be used and integrated in the teaching of the target skill. These strategies may include preventive skill-building exercises and role-play (Proactive Teaching), spontaneous efforts to reinforce positive performance in the skill area (Effective Praise), recognition of negative performance and alternative skill-teaching (Corrective Teaching), and consistent use of rewards and privilege losses that are contingent on the youth's behavior. Other techniques, such as participation in a social skills group, practice with parents or peers, and counseling interventions, may be integrated into this plan as well. Also included are efforts to promote the youth's generalization of the target skill to other situations

and environments where the skill may be used. Since using the target skill in other diverse situations is a key indicator that the youth is learning, caregivers should monitor this area to measure progress.

In applying the various teaching strategies, it is important that the caregivers are clear on such issues as how each technique is to be used and applied, when and how often each strategy will be used, and in what situations the caregivers will use each technique. Again, consistency among the adults working with and caring for the youth is critical.

The team also should develop a monitoring or data collection system to track the youth's performance of the targeted social skill. The emphasis here is to collect sufficient information on the effectiveness of the teaching strategies so that successful techniques can continue and less-productive techniques can be revised.

7. **Follow-up/Revision.** After implementing the skill-based service plan, the team meets to review the service goals that were set for the youth and the progress that has been made. The team compares the youth's current level of functioning in the targeted skill area with the baseline data collected earlier. If there are negative data trends (i.e., the youth has made no progress or demonstrates the skill less frequently than before), the team should review the plan. There may be problems in the way it is being implemented by the caregivers that can be corrected with further training or by further specifying the strategies. Oftentimes, caregiv-

ers, parents, teachers, and other adults need a lot of encouragement and support to respond differently to a youth's behavior. Also, it is important that the person who is directing the intervention consistently monitors the caregivers' social skill instruction to ensure that they are focused on and effectively teaching to targeted social skills.

If it appears the plan has been implemented correctly and has been used long enough to be effective, but there still is no progress, the team can revise specific aspects of the service plan. This could involve changing the frequency of Proactive Teaching and cued practice exercises, revising the consequences that are being offered, or even changing the skill itself. The important part of this process is making such decisions based on concerted observation of the youth's skills and any data that can be collected.

If the data on the youth's learning of the targeted social skill indicates a positive trend (i.e., the youth is meeting improvement goals and showing a degree of generalization), the team may decide to continue to use the current service plan. The team could, however, set a higher goal for performance of the skill, such as having the youth follow instructions nine or 10 out of 10 times instructions are given to them by caregivers, teachers at school, etc. When the goals for this level of performance are consistently being met, the team can decide to move on to the last step of the service planning process and focus intervention efforts on other prioritized skill deficits.

8. **Maintenance.** We know that a youth will not consistently continue to use a

newly learned skill without intermittent reinforcement. In this step, the team devises a specific plan for maintaining and reinforcing the youth's progress. Formal Proactive Teaching and practice sessions can be gradually decreased to only once per week or month, instead of daily as in the original plan, and the use of artificial rewards such as earned tokens/points and privileges may be gradually removed. It is critical during this fading process that the social reinforcement of the youth's use of targeted skills be consistent and frequent. In other words, when the youth demonstrates a positive skill that now no longer earns them tangible positive consequences or privileges, the caregivers still should respond with enthusiastic and meaningful praise. Effective Praise should still be used, but without a tangible reward in the consequence step. Follow-up on the youth's progress should be ongoing and revised as needed. If a youth regresses to an earlier level of skill use, the original plan (or modifications of the plan) can be reinstated.

Additional Assistance in Service Planning

As an additional aid to the service planning process, Appendix C offers a listing of Curriculum skills grouped by behavior problems and Appendix D lists skills by situations. Appendix C provides a quick reference for caregivers who need to identify skills that can be used in the treatment of a youth who is demonstrating behaviors that are characteristic of a particular problem area (e.g., aggressive and antisocial behavior, depression and withdrawal, etc.). The skills listed under a particular problem behavior are those that may positively affect the youth's functioning in that area. Appendix D lists several common situations or circumstances a young person may encounter. The skills listed under each situation are ones that may assist the youth in appropriately responding to the demands of that situation.

In both cases, the decision on which skills are appropriate to teach a particular youth must be based on a functional assessment of a particular youth's needs and abilities. Thus, the listings provided in Appendix C and D are not intended as a "cookbook" for planning the treatment of a young person, but rather as a guide for caregivers in selecting relevant skills to teach the youth.

Another helpful resource is Boys Town's, *Mental Health from Diagnosis to Delivery*. This book contains a series of charts that list social skills you can teach to children and adolescents who require intervention for specific DSM disorders.

Summary

Service planning charts the course for a youth's improvement in the way they think, feel, and behave. Effective service planning considers the many factors that contributed to a youth's present state, the youth's strengths and weaknesses, and the best ways to change negative behaviors and reinforce positive ones. A good service planning process is individualized, positive, and focused on teaching the appropriate social skills, and empowers youth to make good decisions. It also emphasizes the long-term goals of helping youth internalize and generalize social skills.

CHAPTER 7
The Social Skills Curriculum

The 196 skills of the Boys Town Social Skills Curriculum are drawn from the vast number of situational variables young people might encounter as they grow and develop toward independence. Each skill has been task-analyzed into its essential behavioral elements that may include: 1) specific verbal responses; 2) nonverbal behaviors; 3) specific behaviors to omit; 4) behavioral cues and self-instructions; and, in some cases, 5) subclasses of skills that may be learned separately. The focus here is to provide caregivers and teams with a comprehensive resource they can use when developing effective, therapeutic service plans. (Teams can consist of anyone involved in a child's care – parents, therapists, direct-care staff, supervisors, teachers, school principals, counselors, etc. These teams would have the most immediate and consistent means of implementing the service plan.)

The skills in the Curriculum are organized into four groups – **Basic, Intermediate, Advanced,** and **Complex** – according to the perceived complexity associated with the performance of each skill. The degree of difficulty increases from Group 1 (Basic Skills) to Group 4 (Complex Skills), mainly due to the number of component behaviors required to perform the more advanced or complex skills or because of the difficulties of situations associated with those skills.

The nature of many of the component behaviors of the listed skills also changes with increasing complexity. Skills found in the more complex groupings of the Curriculum will be more likely to contain cognitive or "metabehavioral" steps. Examples of these include cues to a youth to identify characteristics of the immediate situation, notice the responses of other people involved, monitor their own responses and feelings, and instruct themself to engage in certain activities. This added area of learning, along with the specific behavioral responses previously taught by the caretaker, greatly increases the youth's repertoire of skills that can be drawn from in complex and demanding situations.

The Social Skills Curriculum is structured so that the last group is likely to include skills that have many more of these cognitive-based component steps, whereas the first group could be considered more "basic" behavioral skills. Many youth in intervention programs typically begin learning the basic social skills first, and then advance to the more complex skill areas contained in the higher levels. But this may not always be the case. The idea is not that all youth need to learn the skills from each group in the precise order in which they are categorized, but rather that skills can be chosen from the Curriculum that match each youth's individual behavioral needs, abilities, and intervention issues. The system of groups simply gives the child care staff or teacher some measure of relative complexity when prioritizing skills for a youth.

Likewise, when organizing the Curriculum for a social skills training group, instructors would require some measure of cognitive involvement and difficulty in order to appropriately match the Curriculum content to the abilities of the participants. The appropriate choice of skills to teach a youth or group is critical to the teaching process and the eventual success of the learner. This is especially true when staff members are confronted with particularly difficult or troublesome behaviors from their youth.

In the remainder of this chapter, we list the 196 skills of the Social Skills Curriculum, numbered and grouped according to their degree of complexity. Following the list is a large section where all of the skills are presented with their respective steps. In that section, rationales and helpful hints are offered for each of the eight Basic Skills.

For teachers and others who provide instruction in educational settings, Boys Town offers the books, *Tools for Teaching Social Skills in School* and *More Tools for Teaching Social Skills in School*. These books include lesson plans for teaching specific skills, reproducible skill pages, techniques and examples for blending skill-teaching with academic lessons, ideas for motivating and monitoring behavior, and strategies for increasing parent support and involvement. *Tools for Teaching Social Skills in School* and *More Tools for Teaching Social Skills in School* are available through the Boys Town Press.

Basic Skills Group

Skill 1	Following Instructions
Skill 2	Accepting "No" for an Answer
Skill 3	Talking with Others
Skill 4	Introducing Yourself
Skill 5	Accepting Criticism (Feedback) or a Consequence
Skill 6	Disagreeing Appropriately
Skill 7	Showing Respect
Skill 8	Showing Sensitivity to Others

Intermediate Skills Group

Skill 9	Accepting Apologies from Others
Skill 10	Accepting Compliments
Skill 11	Accepting Consequences
Skill 12	Accepting Decisions of Authority
Skill 13	Agreeing to Disagree
Skill 14	Answering the Phone
Skill 15	Asking for Clarification
Skill 16	Asking for Help
Skill 17	Asking for Permission
Skill 18	Asking for Time to Cool Down
Skill 19	Asking Questions
Skill 20	Being on Time (Promptness)
Skill 21	Checking In (Checking Back)
Skill 22	Choosing Appropriate Words
Skill 23	Closing a Conversation
Skill 24	Completing Homework
Skill 25	Completing a Task
Skill 26	Complying with a Reasonable Request
Skill 27	Contributing to a Discussion (Joining in a Conversation)
Skill 28	Correcting Another Person (Giving Criticism/Feedback)
Skill 29	Doing Good Quality Work
Skill 30	Following Rules
Skill 31	Following Written Instructions
Skill 32	Getting Another Person's Attention
Skill 33	Getting the Teacher's Attention

Skill 34   Giving Compliments

Skill 35   Greeting Others

Skill 36   Ignoring Distractions

Skill 37   Initiating a Conversation

Skill 38   Interrupting Appropriately

Skill 39   Introducing Others

Skill 40   Listening to Others

Skill 41   Maintaining a Conversation

Skill 42   Maintaining an Appropriate Appearance

Skill 43   Maintaining Personal Hygiene

Skill 44   Making an Apology

Skill 45   Making a Request (Asking a Favor)

Skill 46   Making a Phone Call

Skill 47   Making Positive Self-Statements

Skill 48   Making Positive Statements about Others

Skill 49   Offering Assistance or Help

Skill 50   Participating in Activities

Skill 51   Refraining from Possessing Contraband or Drugs

Skill 52   Reporting Emergencies

Skill 53   Reporting Other Youths' Behavior (Peer Reporting)

Skill 54   Resisting Peer Pressure

Skill 55   Responding to Persons of Authority

Skill 56   Saying Goodbye to Guests

Skill 57   Saying "No" Assertively

Skill 58   Seeking Positive Attention

Skill 59   Sharing Something

Skill 60   Showing Appreciation

Skill 61   Showing Interest

Skill 62   Staying on Task

Skill 63   Sticking Up for Others

Skill 64   Sticking Up for Yourself

Skill 65   Switching from One Task to Another

Skill 66   Using an Appropriate Voice Tone (or Level)

Skill 67   Using Anger Control (Self-Control) Strategies

Skill 68   Using Structured Problem-Solving (SODAS)

Skill 69   Using Table Etiquette

Skill 70   Volunteering

Skill 71   Waiting Your Turn

Skill 72   Working with Others

Advanced Skills Group

Skill 73   Accepting Defeat or Loss

Skill 74   Accepting Help or Assistance

Skill 75   Accepting Winning Appropriately

Skill 76   Adjusting Behavior Based on Social Cues

Skill 77   Advocating for Yourself

Skill 78   Analyzing Social Situations

Skill 79   Analyzing Tasks to Be Completed

Skill 80   Being Prepared for an Interaction with Law Enforcement

Skill 81   Being Prepared for Class

Skill 82   Being Safe Online

Skill 83   Borrowing from Others

Skill 84   Caring for the Property of Others

Skill 85   Caring for Your Own Belongings

Skill 86   Choosing Appropriate Clothing

Skill 87   Choosing Appropriate Friends

Skill 88   Communicating Honestly

Skill 89   Complying with School Dress Code

Skill 90   Compromising with Others

Skill 91   Concentrating on a Subject or Task

Skill 152   Using Relaxation Strategies

Skill 153   Using Self-Talk or Self-Instruction

Skill 154   Using Spontaneous Problem-Solving

Skill 155   Using Study Skills

Skill 156   Using Technology Appropriately

Skill 157   Working Independently

Complex Skills Group

Skill 158   Accepting Yourself

Skill 159   Altering Your Environment

Skill 160   Asking for Advice

Skill 161   Assessing Your Own Abilities

Skill 162   Being an Appropriate Role Model

Skill 163   Being a Consumer

Skill 164   Being Assertive

Skill 165   Being Patient

Skill 166   Budgeting and Managing Money

Skill 167   Clarifying Values and Beliefs

Skill 168   Differentiating Friends from Acquaintances

Skill 169   Displaying Appropriate Control

Skill 170   Expressing Empathy and Understanding for Others

Skill 171   Expressing Grief

Skill 172   Formulating Strategies

Skill 173   Gathering Information

Skill 174   Identifying Your Own Feelings

Skill 175   Interrupting or Changing Negative or Harmful Thoughts

Skill 176   Interviewing for a Job

Skill 177   Laughing at Yourself

Skill 178   Maintaining Relationships

Skill 179   Making an Appropriate Complaint

Skill 180   Making Moral and Spiritual Decisions

Skill 181   Managing Stress

Skill 182   Planning Ahead

Skill 183   Recognizing Moods of Others

Skill 184   Recognizing Your Own Personal Bias or Opinions

Skill 185   Resigning from a Job or Project

Skill 186   Resolving Conflicts

Skill 187   Responding to Law Enforcement/Police Interactions

Skill 188   Rewarding Yourself

Skill 189   Seeking Professional Assistance

Skill 190   Setting Goals

Skill 191   Taking Risks Appropriately

Skill 192   Valuing Differences

Skill 193   Using Community Resources

Skill 194   Using Leisure Time

Skill 195   Using Self-Monitoring and Self-Reflection

Skill 196   Using Strategies to Find a Job

Basic Skills

1. Following instructions

1. Look at the person.
2. Say, "Okay."
3. Do what you've been asked right away.
4. Check back.

2. Accepting "No" for an answer

1. Look at the person.
2. Say, "Okay."
3. Stay calm (avoid arguing or complaining).
4. If you disagree, ask later.

3. Talking with others

1. Look at the person.
2. Use a pleasant voice.
3. Ask questions.
4. Avoid interrupting.

4. Introducing yourself

1. Look at the person. Smile.
2. Use a pleasant voice.
3. Offer a greeting. Say, "Hi, my name is...."
4. Shake the person's hand (when appropriate).
5. When you leave, say, "It was nice to meet you, [state the other person's name]."

5. Accepting criticism (Feedback) or a consequence

1. Look at the person.
2. Say, "Okay."
3. Stay calm (avoid arguing or complaining).

6. Disagreeing appropriately

1. Look at the person.
2. Use a pleasant voice.
3. Say, "I understand how you feel" or "I hear what you are saying."
4. Respectfully tell why you feel differently.
5. Give a reason.
6. Listen to the other person.

7. Showing respect

1. Obey a request to stop a negative behavior.
2. Refrain from teasing, threatening, or making fun of others.
3. Allow others to have their privacy.
4. Obtain permission before using another person's property.
5. Do not damage or vandalize public property.
6. Refrain from conning or persuading others into breaking rules.
7. Avoid acting obnoxiously in public.
8. Dress appropriately when in public.

8. Showing sensitivity to others

1. Express interest and concern for others, especially when they are having troubles.
2. Treat all people with respect, regardless of race, ethnicity, gender, faith, social status, political affiliation, sexual orientation, ability, or differences.
3. Apologize or make amends for hurting someone's feelings or causing harm.

BASIC – SKILL 1
Following instructions

---

1. **Look at the person.**

Rationale:

Looking at the person shows you are paying attention.

Helpful hints:

- Look at the person as you would a friend.
- Avoid staring, making faces, or rolling your eyes.
- Look at the person throughout your conversation.
- Avoid being distracted.
- Looking at the person will help you understand their mood.

2. **Say, "Okay."**

Rationale:

Saying "Okay" lets the person know you understand.

Helpful hints:

- Answer right away.
- Use a pleasant voice.
- Speak clearly.
- Smile and nod your head (if it is appropriate to do so).

3. **Do what you've been asked right away.**

Rationale:

You are more likely to remember exactly what you're supposed to do if you do it right away.

Helpful hints:

- Complete each step of the task.
- You are more likely to get the work done quickly when you do it right away, and you may be able to get back to what you were doing.
- Stay on task. Don't let other things interfere.
- Do the best job you can.
- If you have problems, ask for help.

4. Check back.

Rationale:

Checking back lets the person know you have followed the instruction.

Helpful hints:

- Tell the person you have finished as soon as you are done.
- Explain exactly what you did.
- Ask if the job was done correctly.
- Correct anything that needs to be done over.
- Some situations may not require you to check back. If you are unsure, always check back.

BASIC – SKILL 2
Accepting "No" for an answer

---

1. ## Look at the person.

Rationale:
Looking at the person shows you are paying attention.

Helpful hints:
- Avoid staring or making faces.
- Refrain from looking away.
- If you are upset, control your emotions. Try to relax and stay calm.
- Listening carefully will help you understand what the other person is saying.

2. ## Say, "Okay."

Rationale:
Saying "Okay" lets the other person know you understand.

Helpful hints:
- Answer right away.
- Speak clearly. Don't mumble.
- Don't sound angry or start to argue. That might lead to problems.
- Take a deep breath if you feel upset.

3. ## Stay calm (avoid arguing or complaining).

Rationale:
Staying calm allows you to hear exactly what the other person is saying.

Helpful hints:

- If you react negatively, you may make the situation worse.
- People will think you are serious about improving if you stay calm.
- Staying calm shows you have control of your emotions.
- Accepting a "No" answer this time may improve the chances of getting a "Yes" answer later on.

4. If you disagree, ask later.

Rationale:

If you disagree right away, you will appear to be arguing.

Helpful hints:

- Take some time to plan how you are going to approach the person who told you "No."
- Plan in advance what you are going to say.
- Accept the answer, even if it is still "No."
- Be sure to thank the person for listening.

BASIC – SKILL 3
Talking with others

---

1. Look at the person.

Rationale:

Looking at the person shows you are paying attention and shows the person you want to talk.

Helpful hints:

- Look at the person as you would a friend.
- Look at the person's face; this will help you understand their mood.

2. Use a pleasant voice.

Rationale:

People won't want to talk to someone who seems unpleasant, angry, or threatening.

Helpful hints:

- Speak clearly.
- Use short sentences that are easily understood.
- Think before you speak.

3. Ask questions.

Rationale:

Asking questions includes the other person in the conversation.

Helpful hints:

- Use open-ended questions to get the other person more involved in the conversation – avoid asking questions that can be answered with only a "Yes" or a "No."

- Ask the person about their opinions, likes and dislikes, and interests.
- Listen intently.
- Be prepared to answer questions the person might ask you.

 ## 4. Avoid interrupting.

Rationale:

Interrupting shows you don't care what the other person is saying.

Helpful hints:

- Make sure the person is done speaking before you respond.
- Maintain eye contact.
- Maintain good posture; don't distract the other person by fidgeting.
- Don't monopolize the conversation or jump from topic to topic.

Introducing yourself

---

1. Look at the person. Smile.

Rationale:

Looking at the person is one way of showing you really want to meet them.

Helpful hints:

- Get the person's attention appropriately.
- Don't stare or make faces.
- Look at the person as you would a friend.
- Looking at the person sets a friendly tone for the beginning of your conversation.

2. Use a pleasant voice.

Rationale:

You will make a good impression if you appear to be friendly.

Helpful hints:

- Speak clearly.
- Talk loud enough to be heard, but not too loud.
- Use proper grammar and avoid slang words.
- Don't interrupt.

3. Offer a greeting. Say, "Hi, my name is...."

Rationale:

Saying "Hi" shows you are friendly and makes the other person feel welcome.

Helpful hints:

- Make sure the person hears you.
- Listen if the other person says anything in return.
- Smile if it is appropriate to do so.

4. Shake the person's hand (when appropriate).

Rationale:

Shaking hands is a traditional way of greeting someone.

Helpful hints:

- Make sure your hand is clean before shaking hands with someone.
- Use a firm grip, but don't squeeze too hard.
- Three shakes is about right when shaking hands.
- Say, "It's nice to meet you" as you shake hands.

    In some cultures or groups, a handshake may not be appropriate. Show respect by honoring cultural traditions.

5. When you leave, say, "It was nice to meet you, [state the other person's name]."

Rationale:

Saying something nice ends your conversation on a friendly note.

Helpful hints:

- Be sincere.
- Use the person's name again when saying goodbye.
- Remember the person's name should you meet again.

Accepting criticism (Feedback) or a consequence

1. Look at the person.

Rationale:

Looking at the person shows you are paying attention.

Helpful hints:

- Avoid staring or making faces.
- Look at the person throughout the conversation. Refrain from looking away.
- Listen carefully and try not to be distracted.
- Paying attention shows courtesy; looking away shows disinterest.

2. Say, "Okay."

Rationale:

Saying "Okay" shows you understand what the other person is saying.

Helpful hints:

- Nodding your head also shows you understand.
- Speak clearly, and try not to mumble.
- By nodding your head or saying "Okay" frequently throughout a long conversation, you let the speaker know you are still listening carefully.
- Use a pleasant tone of voice. Don't be sarcastic.

3. Stay calm (avoid arguing or complaining).

Rationale:

Accepting feedback without arguing shows you are mature.

Helpful hints:

- Stay calm.
- Try to learn from what the person is saying so you can do a better job next time.
- Remember that the person who is giving you feedback is only trying to help.
- If you disagree, wait until later to discuss the matter.

BASIC – SKILL 6
Disagreeing appropriately

---

1. Look at the person.

Rationale:

Looking at the person shows you are paying attention.

Helpful hints:

- Avoid staring or making faces.
- Keep looking at the person throughout your conversation.
- Be pleasant and smile.
- Look at the person as you would a friend.

2. Use a pleasant voice.

Rationale:

The person is more likely to listen to you if you use a pleasant voice.

Helpful hints:

- Speak slowly and clearly. Try not to mumble.
- Use short sentences. They are easily understood.
- Keep a comfortable distance between you and the other person while you are talking.
- Smile. People are more comfortable talking with someone who is friendly.

3. Say, "I understand how you feel" or "I hear what you are saying."

Rationale:

Saying you understand or that you are listening gets the conversation off to a positive start.

Helpful hints:

- Plan what you are going to say before you start to speak.

- If you still feel uneasy about how you are going to start your conversation, practice.
- Start to discuss your concerns as part of a conversation, not a confrontation.
- Be sincere.

4. Respectfully tell why you feel differently.

Rationale:

Using specific words and reasons avoids confusion and gets your point across.

Helpful hints:

- Keeping your voice calm and using detailed facts instead of feelings helps keep the situation from escalating.
- Be prepared to back up what you say.
- If necessary, practice what you are going to say.
- Always remember to think before you speak.

5. Give a reason.

Rationale:

Your disagreement will carry more weight if you give a valid reason.

Helpful hints:

- Be sure your reasons make sense.
- Support your reasons with facts and details.
- One or two reasons are usually enough.
- Remember to stay calm during the conversation.

6. Listen to the other person.

Rationale:

Listening shows you respect what the other person has to say.

Helpful hints:

- Avoid looking away or making faces while the other person is talking.
- Refrain from interrupting.
- Stay calm.
- Don't argue.

Showing respect

1. Obey a request to stop a negative behavior.

Rationale:

When you obey a request to stop a negative behavior, you show you can follow instructions. Being able to follow instructions is one form of showing respect.

Helpful hints:

- By stopping your negative behavior, you may avoid getting into trouble.
- There will always be people who have authority over you. You must do what they say, as long as it keeps you and others safe.

2. Refrain from teasing, threatening, or making fun of others.

Rationale:

By refraining from such behaviors, it shows you understand teasing, threatening, and making fun can be hurtful to others.

Helpful hints:

- If you are always making fun of people or threatening them, you won't have many friends.
- People will think of you only as a tease, not as a nice person.

3. Allow others to have their privacy.

Rationale:

Sometimes people need or want to be alone. You show respect by following their wishes.

Helpful hints:

- Always knock before entering someone's room or a room with a closed door.
- Honor someone's desire to be left alone.

4. Obtain permission before using another person's property.

Rationale:

You have certain possessions that are very important to you. You don't want people using them without permission. When you ask permission to use the property of others, you show that same kind of respect.

Helpful hints:

- Always return items in the same condition as when you borrowed them.
- If you damage a borrowed item, offer to repair or replace it.

5. Do not damage or vandalize public property.

Rationale:

Vandalism and damaging property are against the law. Besides getting into trouble, you show disrespect for your community and country when you vandalize public property.

Helpful hints:

- Accidents do happen, but they always should be reported.
- Offer to replace or repair property you have damaged.

6. Refrain from conning or persuading others into breaking rules.

Rationale:

People will think less of you if you are always trying to take advantage of others or get them into trouble.

Helpful hints:

- If you use people, they won't trust you.
- People don't appreciate being manipulated.

7. Avoid acting obnoxiously in public.

Rationale:

You make a good impression with people when you show you know how to behave and use proper social skills in public.

Helpful hints:

- Be on your best behavior in public. Don't do things like cursing, swearing, spitting, or belching.
- Be courteous to others and mind your manners.

8. Dress appropriately when in public.

Rationale:

When in public, people are expected to look their best. When you live up to this expectation, you show you are mature and understand society's rules.

Helpful hints:

- Being well-groomed and well-dressed makes a good impression.
- Use good judgment when deciding what to wear. Where you are going usually determines what you wear.

Showing sensitivity to others

---

1. Express interest and concern for others, especially when they are having troubles.

Rationale:

If you show interest and concern for others, they are more likely to want to spend time with you or to help you when you need it.

Helpful hints:

- Imagine you are in the other person's shoes. Consider what they might be feeling.
- If you see someone in trouble, ask if you can help.
- Sometimes, just showing you care is enough to help a person get through a difficult time.

2. Treat all people with respect, regardless of race, ethnicity, gender, faith, social status, political affiliation, sexual orientation, ability, or differences.

Rationale:

Being different does not make a person inferior. Treating others with respect shows that you understand everyone deserves to be treated as you would like to be treated.

Helpful hints:

- Every person has different strengths and weaknesses. Strength can be physical, intellectual, emotional, or based on character traits.
- Showing compassion and being available to assist someone in need is a good way to show sensitivity. For example, offer to open the door for someone whose hands are full, or give up your seat on public transportation for someone who is using an assistive device to walk or

stand. If someone does not wish to accept your assistance, calmly accept their decision.

- Avoid staring or making comments.
- Remember that making jokes at the expense of others, particularly related to gender, race, faith, social status, sexual orientation, or ability, is harmful and not acceptable.

3. Apologize or make amends for hurting someone's feelings or causing harm.

Rationale:

Saying you're sorry shows you can take responsibility for your actions and can admit when you've done something wrong.

Helpful hints:

- You can harm someone by what you fail to do, just as easily as by what you do. Some examples are breaking a promise or not sticking up for someone who is being picked on.
- If you hurt someone, apologize immediately and sincerely.

Accepting apologies from others

1. **Look at the person who is apologizing.**

2. **Listen to what they are saying without interrupting.**

3. **Remain calm. Refrain from making sarcastic statements.**

4. **Say, "I accept your apology" or "Thank you for apologizing."**

Accepting compliments

1. **Look at the person.**

2. **Use a pleasant voice.**

3. **Say, "Thank you," "Thanks for noticing," or "I appreciate that."**

4. **Avoid looking away or denying the compliment.**

Accepting consequences

1. **Look at the person.**

2. **Say, "Okay."**

3. **Stay calm (avoid arguing or making excuses).**

4. **If given instructions or suggestions on how to correct the situation, follow them.**

Accepting decisions of authority

1. Look at the person.

2. Listen carefully to the person's decision without interrupting.

3. Avoid arguing or becoming angry.

4. When you have the opportunity to speak, use a calm voice.

5. Acknowledge the decision by saying, "Okay" or "I understand."

6. If appropriate, request a reason or disagree appropriately at a later time.

Agreeing to disagree

1. **Look at the person.**

2. **Calmly state your perspective or opinion.**

3. **Listen with an open mind as the other person states their opinion.**

4. **If the opinion of the other person is hurtful, hold strong to your position, but do not escalate the situation.**

5. **If the other person expresses concerns that appear dangerous to themselves or others, ask for help from an adult.**

6. Understand that people are not always going to agree, and it's important to allow others to think for themselves.

7. If you do not come to an agreement, agree to disagree and calmly end the discussion.

Answering the phone

1. Pick up the phone promptly.

2. Use a calm, pleasant voice to say, "Hi" or "Hello."

3. Listen carefully to the other person.

4. Find the person the caller wants to speak with or offer to take a message.

5. Write the message down and ensure the right person receives it.

6. End your conversation by saying, "Goodbye" or "Thanks for calling," and end the call.

Asking for clarification

1. Look at the person.

2. Ask if they have time to talk.

3. Use a pleasant or neutral voice.

4. State specifically what you are confused about.

5. Listen to the person's reply and ask questions if needed.

6. Thank the person for their time.

Asking for help

1. Look at the person.

2. Ask the person if they have time to help you (now or later).

3. Clearly describe the kind of help you need.

4. Thank the person for helping you.

Asking for permission

1. Look at the person.

2. Use a pleasant voice.

3. Say, "May I please...?"

4. Accept the answer calmly.

Notes: Asking for Permission, Making a Request, and Gaining Consent are three skills that are each used in different situations.

A person generally asks permission to do or use something from a person of authority. For example, you may ask permission to borrow someone's property, to go somewhere with a friend, or to use a hall pass in school.

See Making a Request (p. 131) and Gaining Consent (p. 209) for examples of when and how to use those skills.

Asking for time to cool down

1. Recognize when you are getting frustrated.

2. Get the attention of an adult calmly.

3. Use a quiet voice and ask, "Can I please have a few minutes to calm down?"

4. If the answer is "Yes," use the provided time to practice your relaxation strategies.

5. If the answer is "No," accept the no answer and try to remain calm.

Asking questions

1. **Appropriately get the other person's attention without interrupting. Wait to be acknowledged.**

2. **Look at the person.**

3. **Use a pleasant tone of voice.**

4. **Phrase what you are asking as a question by using words such as "Please," "Would," "What," or "May I...?"**

5. **Listen to the person's answer.**

6. **Thank the person for their time.**

Being on time (Promptness)

1. **Know exactly when you need to be where you are going, and how long it will take you to get there.**

2. **Leave with plenty of time to spare (usually about 5-10 minutes before you would have to leave).**

3. **Go directly to your destination with no diversions.**

4. **When you arrive, check in with someone in authority or with the person you are meeting.**

5. **If you are late, apologize sincerely for not being on time.**

Checking in (Checking back)

1. Promptly return or complete the task.

2. Immediately find the appropriate person to check with.

3. Check in by pleasantly saying, "Here I am..." or "I'm back from...."

4. Truthfully answer any questions about your activities or where you have been.

5. End by saying, "Is there anything else?"

Choosing appropriate words

1. Consider where you are and who you're with.

2. Think about what you want to say and choose words that accurately reflect your thoughts or feelings.

3. Avoid terms which others may find confusing or offensive.

4. If you realize you have offended someone, apologize immediately.

Closing a conversation

1. Change topics only when everyone appears to be done talking about a particular issue.

2. Change to a conversation topic that somehow relates to the previous one, if possible.

3. Allow everyone present a chance to talk about the current topic.

4. If it is time to depart or move to another area, wait for a comfortable break in the conversation.

5. Stand and say, "Excuse me..." or "It was very nice talking to you...."

Completing homework

1. Find out at school what the day's homework is for each subject.

2. Remember to bring home necessary books or materials in order to complete your assignments.

3. Get started on homework promptly, or at the designated time.

4. Complete all assignments accurately and neatly.

5. Carefully store completed homework until the next school day.

Completing a task

1. Listen carefully to instructions.

2. Gather the tools or materials you need.

3. Begin working quickly, carefully, and neatly.

4. Remain focused on the task until it is done.

5. Check your work to make sure you followed all instructions.

6. Check back if appropriate.

Complying with a reasonable request

1. Look at the person making the request.

2. Use a pleasant or neutral tone of voice.

3. Acknowledge the request by saying, "Okay" or "Sure."

4. Promptly complete the requested activity.

5. If you are unable to do so, politely tell the person that you cannot do what they requested.

Contributing to a discussion (Joining in a conversation)

1. Approach the group (or people in conversation) quietly.

2. Look at the person speaking and listen to what is being talked about.

3. Keep a relaxed, attentive posture and nod your head to show interest.

4. Wait for a pause before making any comments.

5. Share something related to the topic, without exaggerating or dominating the conversation.

Correcting another person (Giving criticism/feedback)

1. Look at the person.

2. Remain calm and use a pleasant voice tone.

3. Begin with a positive statement or by saying, "I understand...."

4. Clearly describe your concern.

5. Give a reason.

6. Listen to the person's explanation, avoiding sarcasm, name-calling, or put-downs.

Doing good quality work

1. Find out the exact expectations or instructions for tasks.

2. Assemble the necessary tools or materials.

3. Carefully begin working. Focus your attention on the task.

4. Continue working until the task is completed or criteria are met.

5. Examine the results of your work to make sure it was done correctly.

6. Correct any deficiencies, if necessary. Perhaps, check back with the person who assigned the task.

Following rules

1. Learn what rules apply to the current situation.

2. Adjust your behavior so you are following the rules exactly.

3. Refrain from "bending" rules, even just a little.

4. If you have questions, find the appropriate adult to ask about the rules in question.

Following written instructions

1. **Read the instructions provided completely and carefully.**

2. **Do what the instructions tell you, in the order they are written.**

3. **Avoid changing or skipping any steps.**

4. **If you have questions or need clarification, ask an adult.**

Getting another person's attention

1. Wait until the other person is available.

2. Look at the other person.

3. Say, "Excuse me...."

4. Wait until the person acknowledges you, then say what you want to say.

Getting the teacher's attention

1. **Look at the teacher.**

2. **Raise your hand and stay calm.**

3. **Wait until the teacher looks at you or says your name.**

4. **Ask your question or share your information in a calm voice.**

Giving compliments

1. Look at the person.

2. Use a clear, enthusiastic voice.

3. Praise the person's actions or efforts specifically.

4. Avoid comments that could make others uncomfortable.

5. Give the other person time to respond to your compliment.

Greeting others

1. **Look at the person.**

2. **Use a pleasant voice.**

3. **Say, "Hi" or "Hello."**

Ignoring distractions

1. Avoid looking at the person or thing distracting you.

2. Stay focused on your task or assignment.

3. Resist the urge to respond to distracting questions, teasing, or laughing.

4. If necessary, report the distraction to a nearby adult.

Initiating a conversation

1. **Look at the person or people you are talking with.**

2. **Wait until no one else is talking about another topic.**

3. **Use a calm, pleasant voice tone.**

4. **Ask a question of the other person or begin talking about a new conversation topic.**

5. **Make sure new conversation topics are about appropriate activities and will not offend other people.**

Interrupting appropriately

1. **If you must interrupt a person, stand where you can be seen.**

2. **Wait until the person acknowledges you or signals you to come back later.**

3. **Say, "Excuse me for interrupting, but...."**

4. **Share your request or information quickly.**

5. **Thank the person for their time.**

Introducing others

1. Position yourself near or between the people you are introducing.

2. Use a clear, enthusiastic voice tone.

3. Introduce two people by saying each person's first and last names. For example, say, "Bill, I'd like you to meet Jeff Thompson. Jeff, this is Bill Smith."

4. Allow time for each person to shake hands, greet each other, etc.

5. You also may provide more information about each person to the other (their jobs, schools, where they are from, etc.).

Listening to others

1. Look at the person who is talking and remain quiet.

2. Wait until the person is finished talking before you speak.

3. Show that you heard the person by nodding your head, saying "Okay," etc.

Maintaining a conversation

1. **Look at the person.**

2. **Show the person that you are listening by nodding your head or saying, "Okay."**

3. **Avoid interrupting.**

4. **When it is your turn to speak, use a pleasant voice.**

5. **Ask questions or offer stories/information related to the topic being discussed.**

Maintaining an appropriate appearance

1. Use appropriate daily hygiene skills.

2. Comb your hair.

3. Choose clean clothing that will match your day's activities.

4. Use a moderate amount of make-up, perfume, or cologne.

5. Ask for advice if you are unsure what is proper.

6. Maintain your appearance throughout the day (hair combed, shirt tucked in, etc.).

Maintaining personal hygiene

1. Bathe or shower daily.

2. Brush your teeth in the morning and at bedtime.

3. Brush or comb your hair.

4. Put on clean clothes daily.

5. Wash your hands before meals and after using the bathroom.

6. Put dirty clothes in the hamper.

Making an apology

1. Look at the person.

2. Use a serious and sincere voice.

3. Say, "I'm sorry for..." or "I want to apologize for...."

4. Explain how you plan to do better in the future.

5. If appropriate, offer to make restitution.

6. Thank the person for listening.

Making a request (Asking a favor)

1. **Look at the person.**

2. **Use a clear, pleasant voice.**

3. **Express your request in the form of a question.**

4. **If the person agrees, say, "Thank you."**

5. **If they decline, accept "No" for an answer.**

Notes: Making a Request, Asking for Permission, and Gaining Consent are three skills that are each used in different situations.

Making a request and asking a favor are often used interchangeably, usually between peers. You may ask a friend for a ride to practice or for help with homework, or a neighbor may ask your family to water their plants when they are out of town.

Sometimes, you may make a formal request of an adult, such as asking your supervisor for time off or asking a coach to spend extra time running drills with you (with your parents' permission).

See Asking for Permission (p. 103) and Gaining Consent (p. 209) for examples of when and how to use those skills.

Making a phone call

1. **Accurately identify the number you need to call.**

2. **Dial the number carefully.**

3. **Ask to speak to the person you are calling by saying, "May I please speak with...?"**

4. **Use appropriate language over the phone; no obscenities or sexually suggestive words.**

5. **If the person you are calling is not available, ask the person who answers if they will take a message.**

6. **At the end of your conversation, thank the person for their time.**

Making positive self-statements

1. Identify the things you do well.

2. Share your accomplishments honestly and avoid exaggerating.

3. Begin by saying out loud or to yourself, "I'm proud of…" or "I think I did well at…."

4. Avoid putting down the efforts of others.

Making positive statements about others

1. Try to notice or find out positive things or events about others.

2. Use a clear, enthusiastic tone of voice.

3. Praise a specific trait or ability of the other person, or congratulate them on a recent accomplishment.

4. Avoid saying anything that would invalidate your compliment, such as "It's about time...."

Offering assistance or help

1. Identify when help may be needed.

2. Ask the person if they need help.

3. Listen carefully to their response.

4. If the answer is yes, suggest how you can help and follow through.

5. If the answer is no, respect the answer.

INTERMEDIATE – SKILL 50

Participating in activities

1. Appropriately request to be a part of an activity.

2. Cooperate with others in the group, such as allowing others to take their turns.

3. Use a pleasant voice when talking to others.

4. Remember to accept losing or winning appropriately.

Refraining from possessing contraband or drugs

1. Refuse to accept drugs or contraband from strangers, acquaintances, or peers.

2. Examine your own possessions and decide whether they are appropriate to have (legally, morally, rightfully yours).

3. Turn in drugs or contraband to an appropriate adult or authority figure.

4. Self-report your involvement; peer report, if necessary.

5. Honestly answer any questions that are asked.

Reporting emergencies

1. **Identify exactly what the emergency is.**

2. **Immediately find a responsible adult or police officer, or call 911.**

3. **Specifically state who and where you are.**

4. **Specifically describe the emergency situation.**

Reporting other youths' behavior (Peer reporting)

1. Identify a trusted adult.

2. Look at the person.

3. Use a clear, concerned voice.

4. Describe specifically the inappropriate behavior you are reporting.

5. Give a reason for the report that shows concern.

6. Answer any questions truthfully and be prepared to provide details.

Resisting peer pressure

1. Look at the person.

2. Use a calm, assertive voice tone.

3. State clearly that you do not want to engage in the inappropriate activity.

4. Suggest an alternative activity. Give a reason.

5. If the person persists, continue to say, "No."

6. If the peer will not accept your "No" answer, ask them to leave or remove yourself from the situation.

Responding to persons of authority

1. Look at the person.

2. Use a neutral voice tone when talking.

3. If given an instruction, remain calm and do not argue.

4. Say, "Okay."

5. Do task right away.

Note: If the instruction makes you feel unsafe or puts you or another person in harm's way, share your concern in a calm way with the person giving the instruction. Seek assistance from another person of authority or a caring adult if necessary.

Saying Goodbye to Guests

1. **Stand up and accompany guests to the door.**

2. **Look at the person.**

3. **Use a pleasant voice tone.**

4. **Extend your hand and shake hands firmly.**

5. **Say, "Goodbye, thank you for visiting" or "Goodbye [name], it was nice to meet you."**

6. **Ask the guests to return in the future.**

Saying "No" assertively

1. **Look at the person.**

2. **Use a clear, firm voice tone.**

3. **Say, "No, I don't want...."**

4. **Request that the person leave you alone.**

5. **Remain calm, but serious.**

6. **If necessary, remove yourself from the situation.**

Seeking positive attention

1. Wait until the adult or authority figure has time to attend to you.

2. Look at the person.

3. Wait for acknowledgment.

4. Appropriately ask for time to talk.

5. Discuss positive events or activities.

6. Do not seek attention by whining, pouting, or begging.

Sharing something

1. Let the other person use the item first.

2. Ask the person if you can use it after they are finished with it.

3. When offered the item, use it for a reasonable amount of time, then give it back or offer it to another person.

Showing appreciation

1. **Look at the person.**

2. **Use a pleasant, sincere voice.**

3. **Say, "Thank you for..." and specifically describe what you appreciate.**

4. **Give a reason why what the person did was so beneficial.**

5. **Offer to return the favor or help the person in the future (if appropriate).**

Showing interest

1. Look at the person who is talking.

2. Give quiet acknowledgments, such as nodding your head or saying, "Uh-huh."

3. Acknowledge specifically by saying, "That's interesting."

4. Ask follow-up questions for more information.

Staying on task

1. Look at your task or assignment.

2. Think about the steps needed to complete it.

3. Focus all your attention on what needs to be done.

4. Begin the task immediately and ignore any distractions and interruptions.

5. Work until you are finished or instructed to transition.

Sticking up for others

1. **Look at the situation and identify behaviors of concern.**

2. **Look at the person.**

3. **Using a firm but calm voice tone, state specifically which behaviors are unacceptable and need to stop.**

4. **If behavior continues, remove yourself and encourage others to remove themselves from the situation.**

5. **Ask for help from a trusted adult.**

Sticking up for yourself

1. Remain calm.

- Take a deep breath to relax tension.

2. Look at the person.

- This shows you have confidence and demonstrates respect.

3. Calmly state your opinion or feelings.

- Keep your voice tone appropriate and controlled.
- Be brief and clear.
- Do not attack the other person.

4. Listen to the other's viewpoint with an open mind.

- Consider what their thoughts and feelings may be.
- Think about what may be going on with them (i.e., what might their story be?).

5. Calmly walk away.

Switching from one task to another

1. Be prepared for a change to occur.

2. Look or listen for a cue to change tasks.

3. Leave your current task immediately.

4. Shift your focus to the new task quickly.

5. Stay focused on the new task until finished or given different instructions.

Using an appropriate voice tone (or level)

1. Listen to the level of the voices around you.

2. Change your voice level to match.

3. Watch and listen for visual or verbal cues and adjust your voice if needed.

Using anger control (self-control) strategies

1. When someone or something makes you angry, pay attention to how your body is reacting.

2. Breathe slowly and deeply.

3. Instruct yourself to relax any tense muscles.

4. Ask for a few minutes alone to focus on calming down (if needed).

5. If calming down is difficult, ask a trusted person for help.

Using structured problem-solving (SODAS)

1. Define the problem **S**ituation.

2. Generate two or more **O**ptions.

3. Look at each option's potential **D**isadvantages.

4. Look at each option's potential **A**dvantages.

5. Decide on the best **S**olution.

Using table etiquette

1. Sit quietly at the table with your hands in your lap.

2. Place your napkin in your lap.

3. Offer food and beverages to guests first.

4. When requesting food, remember to say, "Please" and "Thank you."

5. Engage in appropriate mealtime conversation topics.

6. Avoid belching, taking large bites of food, talking with your mouth full, or grabbing food with your fingers.

7. When you've finished eating, ask permission to be excused and offer to clear your guests' plates.

Volunteering

1. Look at the person.

2. Use a clear, enthusiastic voice tone.

3. Ask to volunteer for a specific activity or task.

4. Thank the person and check back when the task is completed.

Waiting your turn

1. Sit or stand quietly.

2. Keep your body still.

3. Stay calm (avoid sighing, whining, or begging).

4. Participate in the activity when invited.

5. Thank the person who gives you a turn.

Working with Others

1. Identify the task to be completed.

2. Assign parts of the task to each person.

3. Discuss ideas in a calm, quiet voice and let everyone share their ideas.

4. Work on tasks until completed.

Accepting defeat or loss

1. Look at the person or members of the team who won.

2. Remain calm and positive.

3. Say, "Good game" or "Congratulations."

4. Reward yourself for trying your hardest.

Accepting help or assistance

1. **Look at the person.**

2. **If help is needed, say, "Yes, thank you."**

3. **If help is not needed, politely say, "No, thank you."**

Accepting winning appropriately

1. **Look at the person or members of the team who lost.**

2. **Remain pleasant but not overly happy or celebratory.**

3. **Congratulate the other person or team for a good game and for trying.**

4. **Avoid bragging or boasting about winning.**

Adjusting behavior based on social cues

1. Look at the person.

2. See what the other person's facial expression or body language looks like.

3. If the person is pleased or interested in what is occurring, continue.

4. If the person is displeased or uninterested in what is occurring, adjust your behavior (such as changing the conversation, altering your own body language or facial expressions, or suggesting an alternate activity).

5. If the person's mood or interest is unclear, politely ask if they would like to continue, or do something different.

Advocating for yourself

1. **Identify a situation in which you should advocate for yourself.**

2. **Remember to remain calm and use a pleasant or neutral voice tone.**

3. **Describe your point of view or the outcome you desire.**

4. **Give rationales for advocating for yourself.**

5. **Thank the person for listening.**

Analyzing social situations

1. **Think about the people you are getting ready to encounter.**

2. **Look at the situation that is occurring.**

3. **Think about appropriate behaviors you have learned in the past.**

4. **Choose the behaviors that seem the most appropriate for the situation and people you are dealing with.**

Analyzing tasks to be completed

1. Make sure you understand the task or assignment.

2. Identify the steps needed to complete the task.

3. Determine what should be done first, second, third, etc.

4. Complete the steps in order.

Being prepared for an interaction with law enforcement

1. Become educated about the role of law enforcement in community safety.

2. Become educated about your rights and responsibilities when interacting with law enforcement.

3. As a citizen, understand your role in keeping your community safe.

4. Understand that fear of police/law enforcement can be a real feeling, and you should ask for help to address those concerns.

5. Ask for help and become educated on behaviors needed to interact with law enforcement in a safe manner.

Being prepared for class

1. Gather all necessary books, papers, homework, and writing implements.

2. Be on time for class.

3. Present homework and assignments when the teacher asks for them.

4. Write down assignments and homework to complete.

Being safe online

1. Follow the rules and guidelines set out for you by the adult (time and location to access, length of time to be online).

2. Access only appropriate websites or computer files (avoid illegal websites that promote violence, hatred, intolerance of others, or are sexually graphic).

3. Communicate honestly but never share your personal information (full name, age, school, phone number, address, bank account, or credit card number) with a stranger.

4. Never meet a stranger you met online without first discussing it with a trusted adult (and never meet a stranger in a private place).

5. Use the skill of peer reporting or self-reporting if you run across a dangerous or harmful situation, or are approached online by a stranger.

6. In uncomfortable situations, always ask a trusted adult for help.

Borrowing from others

1. **Appropriately ask to borrow something from another person.**

2. **Accept "No" if the person declines.**

3. **If the person agrees, find out when you need to return the possession you are borrowing.**

4. **Care for the property of others while you have it and promptly return it when you are finished.**

Caring for the property of others

1. Before using something belonging to another person, ask their permission.

2. Use the item as it is supposed to be used or according to their instructions.

3. Take care of the property as if it were your own.

4. If something gets broken, apologize and offer to repair or replace it.

Caring for your own belongings

1. Use your own property as it is supposed to be used or according to instructions.

2. Avoid needlessly tearing, writing on, or breaking your possessions.

3. When you're done, return possessions to the appropriate place.

4. If something gets broken, tell an adult.

Choosing appropriate clothing

1. Think about what situations and activities will occur during the day.

2. Choose clothing that suits the season.

3. Match colors and styles.

4. Do not wear clothing that is too revealing or associated with gang activities, alcohol, drugs, or smoking/vaping.

5. Care for your clothing throughout the day. Do not cut, tear, or write on clothing.

Choosing appropriate friends

1. **Think of the qualities and interests you would look for in a friend.**

2. **Look at the strengths and weaknesses of potential friends.**

3. **Match the characteristics of potential friends with activities and interests you would share.**

4. **Avoid peers who are involved with drugs, gangs, or breaking the law.**

Communicating honestly

1. Look at the person.

2. Use a clear voice and avoid hesitating.

3. Share information, including all important facts and details.

4. Respond calmly to any questions.

5. Take responsibility for your behavior.

Complying with school dress code

1. Know the clothing limits of your school.

2. Choose clothing that matches those limits.

3. Do not tear or write on your clothing at school.

4. Do not change what you are wearing to school (add or subtract clothing) without telling the adults who are responsible for you.

Compromising with others

1. Identify disagreements before they get out of hand.

2. Suggest alternative activities you and your peer could agree to do.

3. Listen to what your peer suggests.

4. Remain calm and continue to talk about a compromise.

Concentrating on a subject or task

1. Promptly begin work on a task.

2. Focus your attention directly on the subject.

3. If your attention wanders, instruct yourself to concentrate on the task.

4. Ignore distractions or interruptions by others.

5. Remain on task until the work is completed.

Contributing to group activities

---

1. Appropriately request to join in an activity.

2. Ask what role you can play.

3. Do your job thoroughly and completely.

4. Cooperate with others by listening and accepting feedback.

5. Praise the performance of others and share credit for the outcome.

Controlling eating habits

1. **Eat mainly at mealtimes and limit between-meal snacks.**

2. **Eat slowly, putting your knife and fork down between bites.**

3. **Limit yourself to reasonable portions and few second helpings.**

4. **Do not eat impulsively or when you are anxious or frustrated.**

5. **Ask for help from a caring adult if eating habits get out of control.**

Controlling emotions

1. **Learn what situations cause you to lose control or make you angry.**

2. **Monitor the feelings you have in stressful situations.**

3. **Instruct yourself to breathe deeply and relax when stressful feelings begin to arise.**

4. **Reword angry feelings so they can be expressed appropriately and calmly to others.**

5. **Praise yourself for controlling emotional outbursts.**

Controlling the impulse to lie

1. Identify untrue statements before you say them.

2. Stop talking and pause.

3. Answer all questions factually and make only truthful statements.

4. Consider the long-term consequences of lying to others.

5. Apologize for any untrue statements you previously made.

ADVANCED – SKILL 96

Controlling the impulse to steal

1. Identify and avoid situations in which you are likely to steal.

2. Before you steal, stop your behaviors immediately.

3. Instruct yourself to leave the area without stealing.

4. Consider the long-term consequences of stealing.

5. Self-report any previous stealing.

Cooperating with others

1. **Discuss mutual goals or tasks with others.**

2. **Know what you must do to help accomplish those goals.**

3. **Give and accept constructive feedback appropriately with peers.**

4. **Follow rules if you are playing a game and share resources with others.**

5. **Praise peers' efforts and cooperation.**

Coping with anger and aggression from others

1. **Look at the person.**

2. **Remain calm and take deep breaths.**

3. **Use a neutral voice and facial expression; no laughing or smirking.**

4. **Avoid critical or sarcastic comments.**

5. **Listen to and acknowledge what the other person is saying.**

6. **If the other person becomes aggressive or abusive, leave the situation.**

7. **Report the incident to an adult.**

Coping with change

1. Identify exactly what is changing.

2. Ask questions for clarification.

3. Remain calm and relaxed.

4. Appropriately discuss your feelings about the change with a caring adult.

5. Avoid becoming unmotivated or depressed.

Coping with conflict

1. Remain calm and relaxed.

2. Listen to what the persons in conflict are saying.

3. Think of helpful options.

4. If appropriate, offer options to the people who are involved in the conflict.

5. If the situation becomes aggressive or dangerous, remove yourself.

Coping with sad feelings (or depression)

1. Identify what situations tend to make you sad.

2. Acknowledge sad feelings when they arise.

3. Report your feelings to a caring adult or peer.

4. Find alternative activities you enjoy and participate in them. Get outside for fresh air and sunshine.

5. Avoid isolating yourself or withdrawing from friends and relatives.

6. Discuss sad feelings openly and frankly.

Dealing with an accusation

1. **Look at the person with a neutral facial expression.**

2. **Remain calm and monitor your feelings and behavior.**

3. **Listen carefully to what the other person is saying.**

4. **Acknowledge what the person is saying or that a problem exists.**

5. **Ask if this is the appropriate time to respond. Say, "May I respond to what you are saying?"**

6. **If the person says "Yes," respond truthfully and factually by either self-reporting, peer reporting, or honestly denying the accusation.**

7. **If the person says "No," delay your appropriate disagreement to a later time and continue to listen and acknowledge.**

Dealing with being left out

1. Accurately identify you have been left out or excluded.

2. Remain calm and monitor your own feelings and behavior.

3. Either find another positive activity to engage in or locate an adult to talk with.

4. Possibly discuss your feelings with those who initially left you out. Remember to give and accept feedback appropriately.

Dealing with boredom

---

1. **Identify the feeling of being bored.**

2. **Look for alternative, appropriate activities.**

3. **If necessary, request permission to participate in other activities.**

4. **Avoid delinquent, illegal, or gang-related behavior.**

Dealing with contradictory messages

---

1. Identify which messages or people appear to contradict themselves.

2. Ask each person for clarification.

3. Specifically explain what messages appear contradictory.

4. Remember to continue following instructions and delay disagreements.

Dealing with embarrassing situations

1. Think ahead to avoid as many embarrassments as possible.

2. When embarrassed, remain calm and monitor your feelings and behavior.

3. Continue to breathe deeply and relax.

4. If possible, laugh at yourself and forget about the embarrassing situation.

5. Otherwise, remove yourself from the situation in order to collect your thoughts and to relax.

Dealing with failure

1. **Accurately identify that you did not succeed in a particular activity.**

2. **Remain calm and relaxed.**

3. **Instruct yourself to control emotional behavior.**

4. **Find a caring adult and discuss your disappointment or other negative feelings.**

5. **Be willing to try again to be successful.**

Dealing with fear

1. Identify what is making you afraid.

2. Decide whether you are in danger or just feeling afraid or intimidated.

3. Remain calm and relaxed. Continue to breathe deeply.

4. Discuss with a caring adult what is causing your fear.

5. Instruct yourself to eventually conquer your fears.

Dealing with frustration

1. Identify feelings of frustration as they arise.

2. Determine the source of these feelings.

3. Breathe deeply and relax when frustrations arise.

4. Discuss frustrations with a caring adult or peer.

5. Find alternative activities that promote feelings of success.

Dealing with group pressure

1. Look at the group.

2. Remain calm, but serious.

3. Assertively say, "No" to inappropriate group activities.

4. If possible, suggest an alternative activity.

5. Remove yourself if pressure continues.

Dealing with rejection

1. **Examine behaviors that may have led to being rejected.**

2. **Remain calm and relaxed.**

3. **Use a neutral tone of voice with the other person.**

4. **Possibly disagree appropriately or give appropriate feedback.**

5. **If rejection continues, remove yourself and engage in alternative activities.**

Delaying gratification

1. Identify what you want or what you want to do.

2. Instruct yourself to stop behaviors inappropriate for the situation.

3. Remain calm and relaxed.

4. Find alternative activities to substitute.

Displaying effort

1. Remain on task and work diligently.

2. Do your best to accomplish tasks to criteria.

3. Inform others of your efforts, if appropriate.

Displaying sportsmanship

1. Play fair and according to the rules.

2. Avoid fighting or criticizing others.

3. Remember to accept winning appropriately without bragging.

4. Remember to accept losing appropriately without pouting or complaining.

5. Thank the other players for participating.

Expressing appropriate affection

1. Identify your relationship with the other person.

2. Determine the appropriate boundary or level of closeness between you and the other person.

3. Choose the appropriate behaviors to match that level of closeness and the situation.

4. Assess the other person's comfort with the situation and your affectionate behaviors.

5. Refrain from using overly physical displays of affection in public or with people you have only recently met.

Expressing feelings appropriately

1. Remain calm and relaxed.

2. Look at the person you are talking to.

3. Describe the feelings you are currently having.

4. Avoid profanity and statements of blame.

5. Take responsibility for feelings you are having.

6. Thank the person for listening.

Expressing optimism

1. Look at the person.

2. Use an enthusiastic voice tone.

3. Describe potential positive outcomes.

4. Express hope and desire for positive outcomes.

5. Thank the person for listening.

Expressing pride in accomplishments

1. Look at the person you are talking to.

2. Use an enthusiastic voice tone.

3. Describe accomplishments and your pride in them.

4. Be careful not to brag, boast, or put down others.

Following safety rules

1. Learn the rules that apply to different situations.

2. Adjust behaviors according to directives in rules.

3. Do not "bend" or test safety rules.

4. Report others who break safety rules, for their own good.

Following through on agreements and contracts

1. **Avoid making commitments you cannot keep.**

2. **Know exactly what is involved in any agreements you make.**

3. **Do exactly what you committed to do, promptly and completely.**

4. **If you cannot follow through, apologize and offer to compensate.**

Gaining consent

1. Look at the person.

2. Use a pleasant voice.

3. Say something like, "Would you like to...?" or, "May I please...?"

4. Accept the answer calmly.

5. If the answer is no, do not beg, persist, pressure, or force the other person.

6. If the answer is yes, understand that consent may be withdrawn at any time, and the decision must be respected.

Notes: Gaining Consent, Asking for Permission, and Making a Request are three skills that are each used in different situations.

Gaining consent is used for personal or serious matters. You need to gain consent to speak on behalf of someone, to find out personal information about someone from a doctor or other professional, or to hug, touch, or have intimate contact with someone.

If someone gives you consent one time, it does not mean that consent is granted every time in the future. Consent must be requested each time you partake in activities like those described above and can be withdrawn at any time. A no answer or withdrawn consent must be respected, and the activity stopped immediately

See Asking for Permission (p. 103) and Making a Request (p. 131) for examples of when and how to use those skills.

Giving consent

---

1. Look at the person.

2. Think seriously about their request. Do not allow yourself to feel pressured or intimidated.

3. If you are not comfortable or interested, confidently say, "No."

4. If you are comfortable and would like to accept the request, say, "Yes."

5. If you change your mind at any time, firmly say, "Stop," "No," or "I've changed my mind."

6. If necessary, remove yourself from the situation by asking the person to leave or by leaving.

Notes: Consent is used when it comes to agreeing to or granting permission related to something very personal or serious. For someone to speak on your behalf, to find out personal information about you from a doctor or other professional, or to hug, touch, or have intimate contact with you, you must first give consent.

When it comes to consent, it's important to be firm and clear in your answers. Think hard about your response in these circumstances.

A yes answer is used when you are comfortable and very interested or eager. A yes answer can become a no answer at any time. Even if you've given consent in the past, you can say no next time.

For example, one day you and a friend may greet each other with a hug, but then another day you may not feel like hugging, so you offer a fist bump, secret handshake, or wave instead. Or, a pregnant woman may be comfortable with a friend touching her belly, but then may change her mind after a few seconds of touching and tell the friend to stop.

A no answer is used when you are certain you don't want to give consent, or if you are unsure about whether you want to. No is a safe way to make sure you have time to think about your options before you give consent to someone.

When you say no, someone may ask for a reason. You may offer a reason if you want to, but you are not obligated to provide a reason in these personal circumstances. A statement such as "I'm not interested in that" or "I'm not comfortable with that" is an acceptable response. If the person persists or attempts to intimidate, pressure, or coerce you, removing yourself from the situation is the best option.

Giving instructions

1. Look at the person you are instructing.

2. Begin with "Please...."

3. State specifically what you would like them to do.

4. Offer rationales, if needed.

5. Thank the person for listening and for following your instructions.

Giving rationales

---

1. Look at the person.

2. Explain your point of view with rationales the other person can understand.

3. Use rationales that point out the potential benefit to the other person.

4. Ask if the person understands your reasoning.

Keeping property in its place

1. Know where property is usually kept or belongs.

2. Ask the appropriate person for permission to remove property.

3. Take care of property you are responsible for.

4. Return the property to its place in its original condition.

Lending to others

1. If possible, respond to requests of others by saying, "Yes."

2. Lend only your property or things for which you are responsible.

3. Specify when you would like your property returned.

4. Thank the other person for returning your property.

Making decisions

1. Accurately identify what decision you must make.

2. Examine what your choices currently appear to be.

3. Generate other choices, if possible.

4. Look at the potential consequences (positive and negative) of each choice.

5. Pick the first- and second-best choices based on the potential outcomes.

Making new friends

1. Look at the potential new friend.

2. Use a pleasant voice and introduce yourself.

3. Share some of your interests and hobbies.

4. Listen to the other person's name and areas of interest.

5. Plan appropriate activities with permission.

Making restitution (Compensating)

1. Begin by making an appropriate apology.

2. Offer to compensate for any offenses you may have committed.

3. Follow through on restitution promises.

4. Thank the person for allowing you to make compensation.

Managing time

1. **List all tasks for a particular day or week.**

2. **Estimate the time needed to complete each task.**

3. **Plan for delays, setbacks, and problems.**

4. **Implement a daily schedule that includes planned tasks.**

5. **Evaluate your time-management plan for effectiveness.**

Negotiating with others

1. **Calmly explain your viewpoint to the other person.**

2. **Listen to the other person's ideas.**

3. **Offer an alternative or compromise that is mutually beneficial.**

4. **Give rationales for opinions.**

5. **Together choose the best alternative.**

6. **Thank the person for listening.**

Organizing tasks and activities

1. List all tasks you are required to do.

2. Prioritize tasks based on importance and your abilities and time.

3. Complete tasks in the order of priority.

4. Manage your time well and avoid putting off tasks until the last minute.

Persevering on tasks and projects

1. **Know exactly what must be done in order to complete a task or project.**

2. **Get started promptly without procrastinating.**

3. **Remain on task until finished.**

4. **Deal appropriately with frustrations or disappointments.**

ADVANCED – SKILL 134
Planning meals

1. **Know what food is available or make a grocery list.**

2. **Plan meals based on the four food groups.**

3. **If necessary, ask for suggestions or feedback from roommates.**

4. **Monitor the contents of foods you buy. Avoid foods high in fats and carbohydrates.**

Preparing for a stressful conversation

1. Remember and practice relaxation strategies.

2. Instruct yourself to continue breathing deeply.

3. Remember to keep looking at the person and express your feelings appropriately.

4. Review skills such as Accepting Criticism (Feedback) or a Consequence, Disagreeing Appropriately, and Solving Problems.

Preventing trouble with others

1. **Identify situations that commonly result in conflicts.**

2. **Review the skills necessary to handle those specific situations.**

3. **Approach situations with a positive voice, a smile, and a willingness to compromise.**

4. **Ask for advice from a caring adult.**

Problem-solving a disagreement

1. Look at the person.

2. Remain calm. Use a pleasant voice.

3. Identify options for solving the disagreement.

4. Consider the potential consequences.

5. Choose the best solution for the situation.

6. Be open to the other person's views.

Reading social cues

1. **Look at the person.**

2. **Observe the person's facial expressions (smile, frown, position of eyebrows, eye contact or no eye contact, etc.).**

3. **Pay attention to the person's body language (sitting up straight, slumping posture, arms crossed, facing you or turning away, etc.).**

4. **Think about what the other person's behavior might mean (smiling, eyebrows raised, eye contact, facing you, and arms open may indicate they are pleased or interested; frowning, looking away, eyebrows furrowed, and turning away may mean they are displeased or uninterested).**

Responding to complaints

1. **Look at the person.**

2. **Remain calm.**

3. **Listen closely to the person's complaint.**

4. **Express empathy and acknowledge the problem.**

5. **If appropriate, apologize and attempt to correct the problem.**

6. **Delay disagreements until later.**

Responding to the feelings of others

1. Listen closely to the other person.

2. Acknowledge what they are saying and feeling.

3. Express concern and empathy.

4. Offer to help or provide advice, if the other person wants it.

5. Encourage the person to seek additional help, if necessary.

Responding to the humor of others

1. If the humor is appropriate, laugh accordingly.

2. If the humor is inappropriate, ignore it or prompt the person not to make such jokes.

3. If inappropriate humor continues, report the other person's behavior to an adult.

Responding to teasing that's hurtful

1. Remain calm, but serious.

2. Assertively ask the person to stop teasing.

3. If the teasing doesn't stop, ignore the other person or remove yourself.

4. If the teasing stops, thank the other person for stopping and explain how teasing makes you feel.

5. Report continued teasing or hazing to an adult.

Notes: Teasing can be done in a fun way between friends. This type of teasing adds to your friendship. But some teasing is hurtful. Continued teasing and hazing can be a type of bullying. Distinguishing between a mean tease and a fun tease can be difficult. If you are unsure, talk with a trusted friend or adult to help get clarity.

Responding to written requests

1. Read the request completely.

2. Ask for clarification, if needed.

3. Perform the requests promptly and thoroughly.

4. Check back when the task is completed.

Self-correcting your own behaviors

1. Monitor your behaviors during difficult or stressful circumstances.

2. Notice the effects your behaviors have on other people. Notice their response to what you say.

3. Instruct yourself to correct behaviors that appear to make others uncomfortable.

4. Use new behaviors and note their effects.

5. Continue to make adjustments, as necessary.

6. Reward yourself for correcting your own behaviors.

Self-reporting your own behaviors

1. Identify the behavior you feel needs to be reported.

2. Look at the person.

3. Remain calm and use a neutral voice.

4. Describe the behaviors you are reporting honestly and avoid making excuses.

5. Respond to any questions without hesitating.

6. Include others in your report if needed.

Setting appropriate boundaries

1. Imagine a series of circles radiating out from you. Each represents a boundary.

2. Picture people you encounter in one of the circles, depending on the level of closeness with which you and another person are comfortable.

3. Disclose personal information only to those in the closest boundaries.

4. Touch others only in ways appropriate to your boundaries. Also, respect the boundaries of others.

Sharing attention with others

1. Sit or stand quietly while sharing attention.

2. Avoid distracting behaviors such as whining, laughing loudly, or complaining.

3. Wait until others pause before speaking or participating.

4. Contribute to the discussion or activity appropriately.

Sharing personal experiences

1. Decide if you should share personal experiences with the other person.

2. Determine whether that person appears comfortable with what you are telling them.

3. Share experiences appropriate for another person to know.

4. If what you told the other person is confidential, make sure they know that.

Suggesting an activity

1. Get the other person's attention.

2. Suggest a specific activity or project to engage in.

3. Give rationales for your ideas.

4. Listen to the other person's opinions.

Using appropriate humor

1. Use humor only under appropriate circumstances.

2. Avoid humor that makes fun of groups in society, person's abilities or disabilities, or individuals in your peer group.

3. Avoid sexually-oriented jokes and profanity.

4. If humor offends others, promptly and sincerely apologize.

Using appropriate language

1. Choose words that accurately reflect your thoughts and feelings.

2. Avoid making blaming statements.

3. Know the meaning of words and phrases you choose.

4. Avoid profanity, slang, or terms others may find offensive.

5. Frequently ask if you are being clear and understood.

Using relaxation strategies

1. Breathe deeply and completely.

2. Tighten and relax any tense body areas.

3. Instruct yourself to remain calm.

4. Visualize a relaxing scene (e.g., mountains, walking along a beach, etc.).

5. At the first sign of increasing stress, say to yourself "3, 2, 1, relax" and continue breathing deeply.

Using self-talk or self-instruction

1. Look at what is happening around you.

2. Stop ongoing behaviors that are causing problems.

3. Think of the best alternative behavior to engage in.

4. Instruct yourself to engage in the appropriate alternative behavior.

5. Reward yourself for using self-talk or self-instruction.

Using spontaneous problem-solving

1. Stop ongoing problem behaviors and relax.

2. Define the immediate problem situation you face.

3. Think of alternative actions and strategies.

4. Think of the possible consequences for each option.

5. Choose the best strategy for avoiding trouble and improving the situation.

6. Use the best strategy and assess the outcome.

7. Reward yourself for solving a problem.

Using study skills

1. **Gather the necessary books and materials.**

2. **Focus your attention on the required academic work.**

3. **Make notes of important facts.**

4. **Repeat important points to yourself several times.**

5. **Remain on task, free from distractions (no texting, social media, gaming, or TV).**

Using technology appropriately

1. Follow any rules or expectations set for you related to the use of technology.

2. Access only appropriate or designated programs or websites, avoiding those that promote violence, intolerance, or explicit language and images.

3. Avoid reading or posting negative, harmful, or offensive messages about others and sharing personal information online.

4. If you find yourself in a dangerous or uncomfortable situation, report it to a trusted adult.

Working independently

1. **Start on tasks promptly without procrastinating.**

2. **Remain on task without being reminded.**

3. **Continue working unprompted until the task is completed.**

4. **Check back with the person who assigned the task.**

Accepting yourself

---

1. Accurately identify your own strengths and weaknesses.

2. Express appropriate pride in your accomplishments.

3. Compensate for weaknesses by accentuating your strengths.

4. Use self-accepting phrases when talking about your tastes, style, etc.

Altering your environment

1. **Identify situations in which you encounter difficulty.**

2. **Look for parts of those situations that could be changed to bring about improvement.**

3. **Make appropriate changes to improve self-esteem, behavior, and performance.**

Asking for advice

---

1. **Identify a person who is qualified to give you advice.**

2. **Ask the person if they have time to talk.**

3. **Specifically describe the situation in which you need help.**

4. **Listen closely to the advice.**

5. **Thank the person for their time.**

6. **If the advice appears useful, implement the suggestions.**

Assessing your own abilities

1. Make a list of your strengths and weaknesses.

2. List situations in which you have been successful or have had problems.

3. Plan future activities in consideration of your abilities.

Being an appropriate role model

1. **Identify a situation requiring you to appropriately model behavior for younger peers or siblings.**

2. **Engage in positive interactions with adults or peers. Initiate only appropriate conversation topics.**

3. **Refrain from inappropriate language, sexual behavior, delinquency, bullying, etc.**

4. **Correct peer behavior in a positive, constructive manner.**

5. **Remember that inappropriate role-modeling can negatively affect younger children.**

Being a consumer

1. **Know the contents of food and beverages you buy.**

2. **Look for ways to save money through sales, buying store brands, using coupons, etc.**

3. **If a store sells you a defective product, return it and appropriately request a refund.**

4. **Keep track of receipts, warranties, etc.**

5. **Learn what rights consumers have.**

Being assertive

1. **Look at the person.**

2. **Use a neutral, calm voice.**

3. **Remain relaxed and breathe deeply.**

4. **Clearly state your opinion or disagreement. Avoid emotional terms.**

5. **Listen to the other person.**

6. **Acknowledge their viewpoints and opinions.**

7. **Thank the person for listening.**

Being patient

1. Sit or stand quietly.

2. Wait until your turn or until you are called on.

3. Avoid making loud complaints or becoming angry.

4. Disagree appropriately later on.

Budgeting and managing money

1. Assess your consistent weekly or monthly income.

2. List all of the bills or expenses you have to pay during that time period.

3. Estimate the costs of appropriate leisure time activities and entertainment.

4. Set aside 10% of your income for unexpected needs or to put into a savings account.

5. Stay within the budget you have developed.

6. Refrain from impulsively spending money.

Clarifying values and beliefs

1. Decide what behaviors you consider to be appropriate or inappropriate.

2. Learn how your behavior affects other people.

3. Decide what characteristics about yourself you value and don't want to change.

4. Decide if you have characteristics you do not value and would like to change.

5. Picture the type of person you want to be and how this would affect others.

Differentiating friends from acquaintances

1. For each person you know, think about how long you have known them.

2. Identify the activities you may engage in with each friend or acquaintance.

3. Share personal information only with people you know as close friends.

4. Avoid compromising situations (e.g., accepting rides, dating, and drinking) with people you have known for only a short time.

Displaying appropriate control

1. Monitor your feelings and your verbal and nonverbal behavior.

2. Use relaxation strategies to manage stress.

3. Speak calmly, clearly, and specifically.

4. Accurately represent your feelings with well-chosen words.

5. Use language that will not offend others.

COMPLEX – SKILL 170

Expressing empathy and understanding for others

1. Listen closely as the other person expresses their feelings.

2. Express empathy by saying, "I understand...."

3. Demonstrate concern through your words and actions.

4. Reflect back the other person's words by saying, "It seems like you're saying...."

5. Offer any help or assistance you can.

Expressing grief

1. Find an appropriate person to talk to.

2. Discuss your feelings of grief.

3. Feel free to cry or release hurt feelings as needed.

4. Ask for advice, if needed.

5. If needed, seek professional assistance.

Formulating strategies

1. Decide on the goal or product.

2. Analyze the critical steps in accomplishing the goal.

3. List any alternative strategies.

4. Implement the best plan and follow through to completion.

Gathering information

1. Know your topic or what you need information about.

2. Go to the school or local library, or use appropriate online search engines.

3. Ask for help from library reference staff, if needed.

4. Assemble materials.

5. Write down or copy the information you need.

COMPLEX – SKILL 174

Identifying your own feelings

1. Examine how you are currently feeling.

2. List how your feelings change with different situations and experiences.

3. Monitor your physical feelings and your emotions when you actually encounter these situations.

4. Correctly identify and label various feelings as they arise.

5. Communicate your feelings so they can be understood by others.

Interrupting or changing negative or harmful thoughts

1. Identify the unpleasant or harmful thoughts you find yourself having regularly.

2. Think about the negative consequences these thoughts can have on you or others.

3. Instruct yourself to "stop" or tell yourself, "I'm not going to think about this anymore."

4. Replace the negative thought with a positive, true, or logical statement or a positive distraction or activity.

5. Recognize and acknowledge your progress.

6. If these thoughts persist, speak with a trusted adult.

Interviewing for a job

1. Dress neatly and appropriately for the interview.

2. Introduce yourself enthusiastically to the interviewer.

3. Answer all questions honestly and calmly.

4. Emphasize your strengths, as well as what you would still need to learn.

5. Ask any questions you have about the job at the conclusion of the interview.

6. Thank the person for their time.

Laughing at yourself

1. **Identify a situation that previously may have caused you embarrassment or discomfort.**

2. **Look for the humor in these situations.**

3. **Be willing to laugh at your mistakes or imperfections.**

Maintaining relationships

1. **Frequently ask for feedback from others and be willing to accept it.**

2. **Express concern and appropriate affection.**

3. **Negotiate and compromise on activities.**

4. **Share attention with others and avoid possessive or exclusionary behaviors.**

Making an appropriate complaint

1. Look at the person.

2. Phrase your complaint as an objective problem, not a personal attack.

3. Remain calm and pleasant.

4. Be assertive, but avoid repeating your complaint over and over.

5. Thank the person for their cooperation.

Making moral and spiritual decisions

1. **Identify your values regarding life, sexuality, and intimacy.**

2. **Remember your values should be expressed in your behavior.**

3. **Do not use people for your own personal or sexual gratification.**

4. **Behave in ways that demonstrate your respect for fellow human beings and concern for their needs.**

Managing stress

---

1. Identify situations and/or circumstances that produce stress.

2. Learn your body's responses to stressful situations.

3. Use relaxation cues to overcome stress responses.

4. Generalize these relaxation cues to the situations that tend to cause stress.

5. Reward yourself for using stress-management techniques.

Planning ahead

1. **Know your eventual goal or outcome.**

2. **Identify the sequence in which tasks or objectives need to occur.**

3. **Make plans for completing a task that account for demands on your time.**

4. **Keep future plans flexible so they can be adapted to changing circumstances.**

Recognizing moods of others

1. Notice the situation that is occurring.

2. Note the other person's facial expression, voice tone, and gestures.

3. Think about what feelings you are experiencing when you demonstrate similar behaviors.

4. Assess the other person's current mood or feelings.

5. If possible, check out your assessment with them.

Recognizing your own personal bias or opinions

1. Identify where you may have a bias about someone or something.

2. Identify what may cause the bias.

3. Take steps to learn more about the person or subject.

4. Identify if your bias is impacting your words or actions toward others.

5. Take steps to use words and actions that convey respect for differences.

Resigning from a job or project

1. Find out the required amount of notice to be given.

2. Inform your supervisor calmly and pleasantly of your intention to resign.

3. Give a positive reason.

4. Always give at least the minimum amount of notice required.

5. Avoid walking off a job or leaving under negative circumstances.

Resolving conflicts

1. Take a deep breath and remain calm.

2. Listen to the other person's point of view.

3. Explain why you feel differently in a calm, clear voice and share your reasons.

4. Be flexible and willing to compromise.

5. Listen and discuss the situation until you find a solution.

6. If you are unable to reach an agreement, thank the person for trying to work with you.

Responding to law enforcement/police interactions

1. Look at the person and listen respectfully.

2. If you experience fear or discomfort, remain calm and do not escalate behavior.

3. Keep your hands visible to officer.

4. Make a request and wait for affirmation to obtain an object before reaching (i.e., driver's license, insurance information, or something in a compartment or pocket).

5. Follow instructions given by officer.

6. You may politely ask for credentials of officer if they have not been provided.

7. If you have questions, respectfully ask for officer to clarify and avoid arguing.

8. If you have concerns regarding officer's decision or conduct, do not argue or escalate your behavior. You may contest the decision later in court or by filing a complaint.

9. After the interaction, be sure to complete any follow-up items (i.e., citations, fees, court appearances, concerns).

10. Talk to a trusted person about the interaction.

Rewarding yourself

1. Decide if what you have just done is praiseworthy.

2. If so, tell yourself you have done a good job and feel good about it.

3. Possibly give yourself an extra privilege or treat for a particular success.

4. Prompt yourself about your increasing competency and ability.

Seeking professional assistance

1. Decide if you are having a serious problem or crisis.

2. Identify the type of professional that can help you.

3. Locate one through a referral from a professional you currently know or by doing research.

4. Specifically describe your problem to the person you go to for help.

COMPLEX – SKILL 190

Setting goals

1. Decide on your overall values and lifestyle desires.

2. List the resources you need to fulfill these lifestyle options.

3. Examine the intermediate steps in accomplishing your overall outcome.

4. Establish short- and long-term goals that will help you accomplish the steps necessary for the desired outcome.

Taking risks appropriately

1. Identify new activities that hold reasonable risks.

2. Evaluate whether these risks could be dangerous or have negative consequences.

3. If appropriate, try the new activity and do your best.

4. Ask for a trustworthy adult's advice if you are unsure.

Valuing differences

1. Examine the similarities between you and another person.

2. Take note of your differences.

3. Focus on the interests, traits, and activities you share.

4. Express appreciation and respect for the person as an individual.

5. Identify/demonstrate how you can learn and grow by embracing these differences.

Using community resources

1. **Identify your exact needs.**

2. **Use phone directories, online searches, youth hotlines, and free community pamphlets/bulletin boards to locate available services.**

3. **Ask staff members at community groups or organizations, such as schools, public libraries, YMCA/YWCA, and homeless shelters, for help in identifying community resources.**

4. **Use these resources to contact government agencies, the Salvation Army, other nonprofit agencies, and services that can assist you and ask for the help you need.**

Using leisure time

1. Engage in leisure activities when tasks are completed and with permission.

2. Choose activities that are age-appropriate, healthy, and productive.

3. Develop new interests and hobbies whenever possible.

4. Avoid delinquent, illegal, or gang-related activities.

5. Limit your screen time.

6. Look at resources in the community for entertainment and fun.

Using self-monitoring and self-reflection

---

1. **Think about behaviors you are engaging in and the feelings you are having.**

2. **Correctly identify and label your behaviors and feelings.**

3. **Think about whether these are appropriate for the current situation.**

4. **Identify alternative behaviors or skills that would be more productive.**

Using strategies to find a job

1. Decide on the types of jobs you are qualified for.

2. Look in the newspaper or go online to check current employment ads.

3. Check the phone book for businesses where you can apply for a job. Start at their personnel offices.

4. Check with adults you know about businesses they may be familiar with.

5. Examine ads posted at local employment offices.

Appendices
OVERVIEW AND INSTRUCTIONS TO DOWNLOAD INDIVIDUAL SKILLS

The following appendices are designed to serve as a guide for caregivers in identifying which skills to teach to the youth with whom they work.

Appendix A groups skills by social and emotional learning competencies (self-awareness, self-management, social awareness, relationship skills, and responsible decision-making).

Appendix B lists all skills in the Curriculum by skill type, which overlap executive functions (social, emotional management, academic, moral/ethical, and independent living).

Appendix C lists skills according to behavior problem areas. The problem areas are ones that we believe teachers and caregivers most commonly encounter.

Appendix D categorizes skills by situations. These situation categories cover the most common areas where children need to use skills to function and succeed.

The categories provided in Appendices C and D are not comprehensive and do not cover every possible scenario where skills should or must be taught to young people. The categories that are included were chosen because they represent the most common behavioral and situational areas we experience in our direct work with children and in the training and consultation we provide to teachers and service providers.

Overview and Instructions to Download Individual Skills

Individual skills are available to print and download using the instructions provided below:

ACCESS:
https://www.boystownpress.org/book-downloads

ENTER:
Your first and last names
Email address
Code: **944882tssy976**
Check yes to receive emails to ensure your email link is received

APPENDIX A
Social Skills Grouped by Social and Emotional Learning Competency

Relationship Skills

Skill No.	Skill Name
1	Following Instructions
13	Agreeing to Disagree
17	Asking for Permission
20	Being on Time (Promptness)
21	Checking In (Checking Back)
26	Complying with a Reasonable Request
30	Following Rules
31	Following Written Instructions
42	Maintaining an Appropriate Appearance
51	Refraining from Possessing Contraband or Drugs
53	Reporting Other Youths' Behavior (Peer Reporting)
54	Resisting Peer Pressure
59	Sharing Something
62	Staying on Task
72	Working with Others
76	Adjusting Behavior Based on Social Cues
77	Advocating for Yourself
83	Borrowing from Others
84	Caring for the Property of Others
87	Choosing Appropriate Friends
88	Communicating Honestly
95	Controlling the Impulse to Lie
96	Controlling the Impulse to Steal
104	Dealing with Boredom
110	Dealing with Group Pressure
113	Displaying Effort
114	Displaying Sportsmanship
117	Expressing Optimism
118	Expressing Pride in Accomplishments
120	Following Through on Agreements and Contracts
121	Gaining Consent
122	Giving Consent
125	Keeping Property in Its Place
129	Making Restitution (Compensating)
130	Managing Time
131	Negotiating with Others
132	Organizing Tasks and Activities
133	Persevering on Tasks and Projects
138	Reading Social Cues
142	Responding to Teasing that's Hurtful
143	Responding to Written Requests
148	Sharing Personal Experiences
157	Working Independently
158	Accepting Yourself
161	Assessing Your Own Abilities
162	Being an Appropriate Role Model
163	Being a Consumer
166	Budgeting and Managing Money
174	Identifying Your Own Feelings
176	Interviewing for a Job
180	Making Moral and Spiritual Decisions
191	Taking Risks Appropriately
193	Using Community Resources
195	Using Self-Monitoring and Self-Reflection

Self-Awareness

137 Problem-Solving a Disagreement
138 Reading Social Cues
139 Responding to Complaints
140 Responding to the Feelings
of Others
141 Responding to the Humor of Others
142 Responding to Teasing
that's Hurtful
144 Self-Correcting Your Own
Behaviors
145 Self-Reporting Your Own Behaviors
146 Setting Appropriate Boundaries
147 Sharing Attention with Others
148 Sharing Personal Experiences
150 Using Appropriate Humor
151 Using Appropriate Language
154 Using Spontaneous Problem-
Solving
156 Using Technology Appropriately
158 Accepting Yourself
160 Asking for Advice
162 Being an Appropriate Role Model
164 Being Assertive
165 Being Patient
167 Clarifying Values and Beliefs
168 Differentiating Friends from
Acquaintances
169 Displaying Appropriate Control
170 Expressing Empathy and
Understanding for Others
171 Expressing Grief
175 Interrupting or Changing Negative
or Harmful Thoughts
177 Laughing at Yourself
178 Maintaining Relationships
179 Making an Appropriate Complaint
180 Making Moral and Spiritual
Decisions
183 Recognizing Moods of Others
184 Recognizing Your Own Personal
Bias or Opinions
186 Resolving Conflicts
187 Responding to Law Enforcement/
Police Interactions
192 Valuing Differences

Responsible Decision-Making

Skill No.   Skill Name
1 Following Instructions
2 Accepting "No" for an Answer
5 Accepting Criticism (Feedback)
or a Consequence
6 Disagreeing Appropriately
11 Accepting Consequences
13 Agreeing to Disagree
15 Asking for Clarification
16 Asking for Help
17 Asking for Permission
18 Asking for Time to Cool Down
19 Asking Questions
20 Being on Time (Promptness)
21 Checking In (Checking Back)
22 Choosing Appropriate Words
24 Completing Homework
25 Completing a Task
26 Complying with a
Reasonable Request
29 Doing Good Quality Work
31 Following Written Instructions
36 Ignoring Distractions
42 Maintaining an Appropriate
Appearance
43 Maintaining Personal Hygiene
44 Making an Apology
51 Refraining from Possessing
Contraband or Drugs
52 Reporting Emergencies
55 Responding to Persons of Authority
57 Saying "No" Assertively
62 Staying on Task
67 Using Anger Control (Self-Control)
Strategies
68 Using Structured Problem-Solving
(SODAS)
70 Volunteering
77 Advocating for Yourself
78 Analyzing Social Situations
79 Analyzing Tasks to Be Completed
80 Being Prepared for an Interaction
with Law Enforcement
81 Being Prepared for Class
83 Borrowing from Others

293

Self-Management

Social Awareness

Teaching Social Skills to Youth

APPENDIX B

Social Skills Grouped by Skill Type (Executive Function)

Social

Skill No.	Skill Name
1	Following Instructions
2	Accepting "No" for an Answer
3	Talking with Others
4	Introducing Yourself
5	Accepting Criticism (Feedback) or a Consequence
6	Disagreeing Appropriately
8	Showing Sensitivity to Others
9	Accepting Apologies from Others
10	Accepting Compliments
12	Accepting Decisions of Authority
13	Agreeing to Disagree
14	Answering the Phone
15	Asking for Clarification
16	Asking for Help
17	Asking for Permission
19	Asking Questions
21	Checking In (Checking Back)
22	Choosing Appropriate Words
23	Closing a Conversation
26	Complying with a Reasonable Request
27	Contributing to a Discussion (Joining in a Conversation)
30	Following Rules
32	Getting Another Person's Attention
34	Giving Compliments
35	Greeting Others
36	Ignoring Distractions
37	Initiating a Conversation
38	Interrupting Appropriately
39	Introducing Others
40	Listening to Others
41	Maintaining a Conversation
44	Making an Apology
45	Making a Request (Asking a Favor)
46	Making a Phone Call
49	Offering Assistance or Help
50	Participating in Activities
56	Saying Goodbye to Guests
57	Saying "No" Assertively
59	Sharing Something
60	Showing Appreciation
61	Showing Interest
62	Staying on Task
63	Sticking Up for Others
66	Using an Appropriate Voice Tone (or Level)
68	Using Structured Problem-Solving (SODAS)
69	Using Table Etiquette
70	Volunteering
71	Waiting Your Turn
72	Working with Others
76	Adjusting Behavior Based on Social Cues
77	Advocating for Yourself
78	Analyzing Social Situations
83	Borrowing from Others
84	Caring for the Property of Others
87	Choosing Appropriate Friends
90	Compromising with Others
92	Contributing to Group Activities
97	Cooperating with Others
117	Expressing Optimism
118	Expressing Pride in Accomplishments

Emotional Management

138 Reading Social Cues
139 Responding to Complaints
140 Responding to the Feelings of Others
141 Responding to the Humor of Others
142 Responding to Teasing that's Hurtful
144 Self-Correcting Your Own Behaviors
145 Self-Reporting Your Own Behaviors
147 Sharing Attention with Others
152 Using Relaxation Strategies
153 Using Self-Talk or Self-Instruction
154 Using Spontaneous Problem-Solving
158 Accepting Yourself
159 Altering Your Environment
165 Being Patient
169 Displaying Appropriate Control
170 Expressing Empathy and Understanding for Others
171 Expressing Grief
174 Identifying Your Own Feelings
175 Interrupting or Changing Negative or Harmful Thoughts
177 Laughing at Yourself
179 Making an Appropriate Complaint
181 Managing Stress
184 Recognizing Your Own Personal Bias or Opinions
185 Resigning from a Job or Project
186 Resolving Conflicts
187 Responding to Law Enforcement/ Police Interactions
195 Using Self-Monitoring and Self-Reflection

Ethical/Moral

Skill No.	Skill Name
7	Showing Respect
17	Asking for Permission
29	Doing Good Quality Work
44	Making an Apology
51	Refraining from Possessing Contraband or Drugs

53 Reporting Other Youths' Behavior (Peer Reporting)
54 Resisting Peer Pressure
55 Responding to Persons of Authority
82 Being Safe Online
86 Choosing Appropriate Clothing
88 Communicating Honestly
110 Dealing with Group Pressure
112 Delaying Gratification
114 Displaying Sportsmanship
115 Expressing Appropriate Affection
121 Gaining Consent
122 Giving Consent
125 Keeping Property in Its Place
126 Lending to Others
129 Making Restitution (Compensating)
150 Using Appropriate Humor
151 Using Appropriate Language
156 Using Technology Appropriately
162 Being an Appropriate Role Model
167 Clarifying Values and Beliefs
180 Making Moral and Spiritual Decisions
184 Recognizing Your Own Personal Bias or Opinions
191 Taking Risks Appropriately
192 Valuing Differences

Academic

Skill No.	Skill Name
15	Asking for Clarification
16	Asking for Help
19	Asking Questions
24	Completing Homework
25	Completing a Task
29	Doing Good Quality Work
33	Getting the Teacher's Attention
55	Responding to Persons of Authority
62	Staying on Task
65	Switching from One Task to Another
72	Working with Others
81	Being Prepared for Class
89	Complying with School Dress Code
91	Concentrating on a Subject or Task

Independent Living

APPENDIX C

Social Skills Grouped by Behavior Problems

Aggressive and Antisocial Behavior

Skill No.	Skill Name
1	Following Instructions
2	Accepting "No" for an Answer
5	Accepting Criticism (Feedback) or a Consequence
6	Disagreeing Appropriately
8	Showing Sensitivity to Others
11	Accepting Consequences
13	Agreeing to Disagree
15	Asking for Clarification
16	Asking for Help
17	Asking for Permission
18	Asking for Time to Cool Down
28	Correcting Another Person (Giving Criticism/Feedback)
30	Following Rules
38	Interrupting Appropriately
40	Listening to Others
44	Making an Apology
48	Making Positive Statements about Others
54	Resisting Peer Pressure
55	Responding to Persons of Authority
59	Sharing Something
66	Using an Appropriate Voice Tone (or Level)
67	Using Anger Control (Self-Control) Strategies
68	Using Structured Problem-Solving (SODAS)
72	Working with Others
76	Adjusting Behavior Based on Social Cues
80	Being Prepared for an Interaction with Law Enforcement
90	Compromising with Others
94	Controlling Emotions
98	Coping with Anger and Aggression from Others
102	Dealing with an Accusation
109	Dealing with Frustration
110	Dealing with Group Pressure
116	Expressing Feelings Appropriately
121	Gaining Consent
122	Giving Consent
129	Making Restitution (Compensating)
131	Negotiating with Others
135	Preparing for a Stressful Conversation
137	Problem-Solving a Disagreement
138	Reading Social Cues
144	Self-Correcting Your Own Behaviors
152	Using Relaxation Strategies
154	Using Spontaneous Problem-Solving
156	Using Technology Appropriately
164	Being Assertive
169	Displaying Appropriate Control
170	Expressing Empathy and Understanding for Others
177	Laughing at Yourself
179	Making an Appropriate Complaint
181	Managing Stress
184	Recognizing Your Own Personal Bias or Opinions

68	Using Structured Problem-Solving (SODAS)
83	Borrowing from Others
84	Caring for the Property of Others
87	Choosing Appropriate Friends
88	Communicating Honestly
95	Controlling the Impulse to Lie
96	Controlling the Impulse to Steal
102	Dealing with an Accusation
104	Dealing with Boredom
105	Dealing with Contradictory Messages
110	Dealing with Group Pressure
112	Delaying Gratification
120	Following Through on Agreements and Contracts
125	Keeping Property in Its Place
126	Lending to Others
129	Making Restitution (Compensating)
144	Self-Correcting Your Own Behaviors
145	Self-Reporting Your Own Behaviors
154	Using Spontaneous Problem-Solving
159	Altering Your Environment
165	Being Patient
166	Budgeting and Managing Money
167	Clarifying Values and Beliefs
180	Making Moral and Spiritual Decisions
182	Planning Ahead
190	Setting Goals
194	Using Leisure Time

Peer Interaction Difficulties

Skill No.	Skill Name
2	Accepting "No" for an Answer
3	Talking with Others
4	Introducing Yourself
5	Accepting Criticism (Feedback) or a Consequence
6	Disagreeing Appropriately
8	Showing Sensitivity to Others
9	Accepting Apologies from Others
10	Accepting Compliments
13	Agreeing to Disagree

17	Asking for Permission
22	Choosing Appropriate Words
27	Contributing to a Discussion (Joining in a Conversation)
28	Correcting Another Person (Giving Criticism/Feedback)
32	Getting Another Person's Attention
34	Giving Compliments
36	Ignoring Distractions
40	Listening to Others
43	Maintaining Personal Hygiene
44	Making an Apology
50	Participating in Activities
51	Refraining from Possessing Contraband or Drugs
53	Reporting Other Youths' Behavior (Peer Reporting)
54	Resisting Peer Pressure
57	Saying "No" Assertively
59	Sharing Something
63	Sticking Up for Others
64	Sticking Up for Yourself
66	Using an Appropriate Voice Tone (or Level)
71	Waiting Your Turn
72	Working with Others
73	Accepting Defeat or Loss
75	Accepting Winning Appropriately
76	Adjusting Behavior Based on Social Cues
82	Being Safe Online
83	Borrowing from Others
84	Caring for the Property of Others
87	Choosing Appropriate Friends
90	Compromising with Others
92	Contributing to Group Activities
98	Coping with Anger and Aggression from Others
103	Dealing with Being Left Out
106	Dealing with Embarrassing Situations
110	Dealing with Group Pressure
114	Displaying Sportsmanship
121	Gaining Consent
122	Giving Consent
131	Negotiating with Others
137	Problem-Solving a Disagreement
138	Reading Social Cues

School Behavior and Attendance Problems

Serious Conflicts with Authority Figures

Sexual Behavior

Sexual Perpetrator Behavior

APPENDIX D

Social Skills Grouped by Common Situations

Chronic Relocation and Running Away

Classroom Behavior and Academic Performance

Drug and Alcohol Abuse

Friendship and Dating

Impulse Control Difficulty and Attention Deficits

Interactions with Parents and Family

Interaction with Supervisors and Co-Workers

Interpersonal Conflict and Disagreement

Low Self-Esteem

Meeting or Working with Someone Who Is Different from You

Transition to Independent Living

References

Ang, R., & Hughes, J. (2001). Differential benefits of skills training with antisocial youth based on group composition: **A meta-analytic investigation. School Psychology Review, 31** (2), 164-85.

Arthur, M., Bochner, S., & Butterfield, N. (1999). Enhancing peer interactions within the context of play. **International Journal of Disability, Development, and Education, 46** (3), 367-81.

Ashford, J., & LeCroy, C.W. (2013). **Human Behavior in the Social Environment,** (5th ed.). Belmont, CA: Brooks/Cole.

Baddeley, A.D. (1986). **Working Memory.** Oxford, England: Clarendon Press.

Baer, D.M., & Wolf, M.M. (1970). The entry into natural communities of reinforcement. In R. Ulrich, T. Stachnik, & J. Mabry (Eds.), **Control of Human Behavior, Vol. 2** (pp. 319-324). Glenview, IL: Scott Foresman.

Bandura, A. (1989). Social cognitive theory. In V.R. Greenwich (Ed.), **Annals of child development** (pp. 1-60). Greenwich, CT: Jai Press.

Barkley, R. A. (2012). **Executive functions: What they are, how they work, and why they evolved.** New York: Guilford Press.

Berkowitz, L. (1983). Aversively stimulated aggression: Some parallels and differences in research with animals and humans. **American Psychologist, 38** (11), 1135-1144.

Carter, S. L. (2010). **The social validity manual: A guide to subjective evaluation of behavior interventions.** Oxford, England: Elsevier, Inc.

Cartledge, G., & Kleefeld, J. (2009). **Taking part: Introducing social skills to children,** (2nd ed.). Champaign, IL: Research Press.

Cartledge G., & Milburn, J. F. (1995). **Teaching social skills to children: Innovative approaches,** (3rd ed.). Boston: Allyn and Bacon.

Cartledge, G., & Milburn, J.F. (1996). **Cultural diversity and social skills instruction: Understanding ethnic and gender differences.** Champaign, IL: Research Press.

Center on the Developing Child at Harvard University (2011). **Building the brain's "air traffic control" system: How early experiences shape the development of executive function: Working paper no. 11.** [Online]. Available: http://www.developingchild.harvard.edu.

Centers for Disease Control and Prevention (2019). Youth Risk Behavior Survey Data. Available at: www.cdc.gov/yrbs. Accessed on February 22, 2022).

Collaborative for Academic, Social, and Emotional Learning (2014). **2015 CASEL guide: Effective social and emotional learning programs—Middle and high school edition.** Chicago: Author.

Collaborative for Academic, Social, and Emotional Learning (2020). What Is the CASEL Framework? - CASEL. [Online]. Available: https://casel.org/fundamentals-of-sel/what-is-the-casel-framework. Retrieved February 22, 2022.

Collaborative for Academic, Social, and Emotional Learning (2022). What Does the Research Say? - CASEL. [Online]. Available: https://casel.org/fundamentals-of-sel/what-does-the-research-say. Retrieved February 22, 2022.

Cruickshank, W.M., Morse, W.C., & Johns, J.S. (1980). **Learning disabilities: The struggle from adolescence toward adulthood.** Syracuse, NY: Syracuse University Press.

DeBaryshe, B.D., Patterson, G.R., & Capaldi, D.M. (1993). A performance model for academic achievement in early adolescent boys. **Developmental Psychology, 29,** 795-804.

Dishion, T.J. (1992, October). **An applied model of antisocial behavior.** Paper presented at a workshop for potential applicants for NIMH research grants to prevent youth violence, Bethesda, MD.

Dodge, K.A., Price, J.M., Bachorowski, J., & Newman, J.P. (1990). Hostile attribution: Biases in severely aggressive adolescents. **Journal of Abnormal Psychology, 99,** 385-392.

Elias, M.J., Parker, S.J., Kash, V.M., Weissberg, R.P., & O'Brien, M.U. (2008). Social and emotional learning, moral education, and character education: A comparative analysis and a view toward convergence. In L. Nucci & D. Narvaez (Eds.), **Handbook of moral education** (pp. 248-266). Mahwah, NJ: Lawrence Erlbaum Associates.

Elliott, D.S. (1992, October). **Correlates of youth violence, and designing evaluations of interventions.** Paper presented at workshop for potential applicants for NIMH research grants to prevent youth violence, Bethesda, MD.

Friedman, R.M., Quick, J., Mayo, J., & Palmer, J. (1983). Social skills training within a day treatment program for emotionally disturbed adolescents. In C. LeCroy (Ed.), **Social skills training for children and youth** (pp. 139-151). New York: Haworth Press.

Goldstein, A.P., Sprafkin, R.P., Gershaw, N.J., & Klein, P. (1980). The adolescent: Social skills training through structured learning. In G. Cartledge & J.F. Milburn (Eds.), **Teaching social skills to children** (pp. 249-279). New York: Pergamon Press.

Goleman, D. (2005). **Emotional intelligence: 10th anniversary edition; Why it can matter more than IQ.** New York: Bantam Dell.

Greenberg, M.T., Weissberg, R.P., O'Brien, M.U., Zins, J.E., Fredericks, L., Resnick, H., & Elias, M.J. (2003). Enhancing school-based prevention and youth development through coordinated social, emotional, and academic learning. **American Psychologist, 58** (6-7), 466-474.

Greenspan, S. (2012, March 11). Determining teacher competence: What's wrong with grading teachers? [Web log post]. Retrieved from https://www.psychologytoday.com/blog/incompetence/201203/determining-teacher-competence.

Gresham, F.M. (1981). Social skills training with handicapped children: A review. **Review of Educational Research, 51** (1), 139-176.

Gresham, F.M. (1995). Best practices in social skills training. In A. Thomas & J. Grimes (Eds.), **Best practices in school psychology – III** (pp. 1021-1030). Washington, DC: The National Association of School Psychologists.

Gresham, F.M. (1998). Social skills training: Should we raze, remodel, or rebuild? **Behavioral Disorders, 24** (1), 19-25.

Gresham, F.M., Sugai, G., & Horner, R.H. (2001). Interpreting outcomes of social skills training for students with high-incidence disabilities. **Exceptional Children, 67** (3), 331-344.

Gresham, F.M., Van, M.B., & Cook, C.R. (2006). Social skills training for teaching replacement behaviors: Remediating acquisition deficits in at-risk students. **Behavioral Disorders, 31** (4), 363-377.

Hansen, D.J., St. Lawrence, J.S., & Christoff, K.A. (1989). Group conversation-skills training with inpatient children and adolescents: Social validation, generalization, and maintenance. **Behavior Modification, 13** (1), 4-31.

Hartup, W.W., & Moore, S.G. (1990). Early peer relations: Developmental significance and prognostic implications. **Early Childhood Research Quarterly, 5** (1), 1-18.

Hazel, J.S., Schumaker, J.B., Sherman, J.A., & Sheldon-Wildgen, J.S. (1983). Social skills training with court-adjudicated youths. In C. LeCroy (Ed.), **Social skills training for children and youth** (pp. 117-137). New York: Haworth Press.

Howing, P.T., Wodarski, J.S., Kurtz, P.D., & Gaudin, J.M. (1990). The empirical base for the implementation of social skills training with maltreated children. **Social Work, 35** (5), 460-467.

Kamps, D., Royer, J., Dugan, E., Kravits, T., Gonzalez-Lopez, A., Garcia, J., Carnazzo, K., Morrison, L., & Kane, L.G. (2002). Peer training to facilitate social interaction for elementary students with autism and their peers. **Exceptional Children, 68** (2), 173-187.

Kazdin, A.E. (1985). **Treatment of antisocial behavior in children and adolescents.** Homewood, IL: The Dorsey Press.

Kazdin, A.E. (2001). **Behavior modification in applied settings,** (6th ed.). Belmont, CA: Wadsworth.

Kinsey, S.J. (2000). **The relationship between prosocial behaviors and academic achievement in the primary multi-age classroom.** Unpublished doctoral dissertation. Loyola University, Chicago.

Kurtz, P.D., Gaudin, J.M. Wodarski, J.S., & Howing, P.T. (1993). Maltreatment and the school-aged child: School performance consequences. **Child Abuse & Neglect, 17** (5), 581-589.

Ladd, G.W. (2000). The fourth R: Relationships as risks and resources following children's transition to school. **American Educational Research Association Division E Newsletter, 19** (1), 7-11.

Ladd, G.W., & Profilet, S.M. (1996). The child behavior scale: A teacher-report measure of young children's aggressive, withdrawn, and prosocial behaviors. **Developmental Psychology, 32** (6), 1008-1024.

Lane, K.L., Wehby, J., Menzies, H.M., Doukas, G.L., Munton, S.M., & Gregg, R.M. (2003).

Social skills instruction for students at risk for antisocial behavior: The effects of small-group instruction. **Behavioral Disorders, 28** (3), 229-248.

LeCroy, C.W. (1983). Social skills training with adolescents: A review. In C. LeCroy (Ed.), **Social skills training in children and youth** (pp. 117-137). New York: Haworth Press.

Mayer, G.R. (1995). Preventing antisocial behavior in the schools. **Journal of Applied Behavior Analysis, 28** (4), 467-478.

Mayer, G.R. (2001). Antisocial behavior: Its causes and prevention within our schools. **Education and Treatment of Children, 24** (4), 414-429.

Mayer, G.R., Sulzer-Azaroff, B., & Wallace, M. (2013). **Behavior analysis for lasting change,** (3rd ed.). Cornwall-on-Hudson, NY: Sloan Publisher.

McClellan, D.E., & Kinsey, S. (1997, April). **Children's social behavior in relation to participation in mixed-age or same-age classrooms.** ERIC Document Reproduction Service (EDRS), ED418771. Paper presented at the Biennial Meeting of the Society for Research in Child Development (SRCD), Washington, DC.

McGrady, K.M. (2022). **Mental health from diagnosis to delivery: How to incorporate effective social skills training into treatment plans.** Boys Town, NE: Boys Town Press.

McPhail, J.C. (1993). Adolescents with learning disabilities: A comparative life-stream interpretation. **Journal of Learning Disabilities, 26** (9), 617-629.

Moote, G., Smyth, N.J., & Wodarski, J.S. (1999). Social skills training with youth in school settings. A review. **Research on Social Work Practice, 9** (4), 427-465.

Morin, A. (2014, March). Understanding Executive Function Issues. [Web log post]. Retrieved from https://www.understood.org/en/learning-attention-issues/child-learning-disabilities/executive-functioning-issues/understanding-executive-functioning-issues.

Moyer, J., & Dardig, J.C. (1978). Practical task analysis for special educators. **Teaching Exceptional Children, 3,** 16-18.

National Research Council (2012). **Education for life and work: Developing transferable knowledge and skills in the 21st century.** Committee on Defining Deeper Learning and 21st Century Skills, James W. Pellegrino and Margaret L. Hilton, Editors. Board on Testing and Assessment and Board on Science Education, Division of Behavioral and Social Sciences and Education. Washington, DC: The National Academies Press.

Oden, S. (1980). A child's social isolation: Origins, prevention, intervention. In G. Cartledge & J.F. Milburn (Eds.), **Teaching social skills to children** (pp. 179-202). New York: Pergamon Press.

Parker, J.G., & Asher, S.R. (1987). Peer relations and later personal adjustment: Are low-accepted children at risk? **Psychological Bulletin, 102** (3), 357-389.

Patterson, G.R. (1982). **Coercive family process.** Eugene, OR: Castalia.

Patterson, G.R. (1992). Developmental changes in antisocial behavior. In R.D. Peters, R.J. McMahon, & V.L Quinsey (Eds.), **Aggression and violence throughout the life span** (pp. 52-82). Newbury Park, CA: Sage.

Powers, L.J. (2003). **Examining the effects of targeted group social skills intervention in schools with and without school-wide systems of positive behavior support.** Unpublished doctoral dissertation. University of Missouri, Columbia.

Pribram, K.H. (1973). The primate frontal cortex—executive of the brain. In K.H. Pribram & A.R. Luria (Eds.), **Psychophysiology of the frontal lobes** (pp. 293-332). New York: Academic Press.

Pribram, K.H. (1976). Executive functions of the frontal lobe. In T. Desiraju (Ed.), **The transmission of signals for conscious behavior** (pp. 303-322). Amsterdam: Elsevier Science & Technology.

Robinson, T.R., Smith, S.W., Miller, M.D., & Brownell, M.T. (1999). Cognitive behavior modification of hyperactivity/impulsivity and aggression: A meta-analysis of school-based studies. **Journal of Educational Psychology, 91** (2), 195-203.

Rogoff, B.M. (1990). **Apprenticeship in thinking: Cognitive development in social context.** New York: Oxford University Press.

Shivrattan, J.L. (1988). Social interactional training and incarcerated juvenile delinquents. **Canadian Journal of Criminology, 30** (2), 145-163.

Sklad, M., Diekstra, R., DeRitter, M., Ben, J., & Gravesteijn, C. (2012). Effectiveness of school-based universal social, emotional, and behavioral programs: Do they enhance students' development in the area of skill, behavior, and adjustment? **Psychology in the Schools, 49** (9), 892-909.

Spence, S.H. (2003). Social skills training with children and young people: Theory, evidence, and practice. **Child and Adolescent Mental Health, 8** (2), 84-96.

Spence, S.H., & Donovan, C. (1998). Interpersonal problems. In P. Graham (Ed.), **Cognitive-behaviour therapy for children and families** (pp. 217-245). Cambridge, England: Cambridge University Press.

Sterba, M., & Dowd, T. (1998). **Treating youth with DSM-IV disorders: The role of social skill instruction.** Boys Town, NE: Boys Town Press.

Sulzer-Azaroff, B., & Mayer, G.R. (1986). **Achieving educational excellence using behavioral strategies.** New York: Holt, Rinehart and Winston.

Trower, P., Bryant, B., & Argyle, M. (2015). **Social skills and mental health (psychology revivals).** New York: Routledge.

Vernon, S., Hazel, J.S., & Schumaker, J.B. (1988). Now that the door is open: Social skills instruction in the classroom. **PRISE Reporter, 20,** 1-2.

Walker, H.M., Ramsey, E., & Gresham, F.M. (2004). **Antisocial behavior in school: Evidence-based practices.** Belmont, CA: Thomson/Wadsworth.

Webb, N.L. (2005, November). Alignment, depth of knowledge, & change. **Florida Educational Research Association 50th annual meeting,** Miami, Florida. Retrieved from http://facstaff.wcer.wisc.edu/normw/MIAMI%20FLORIDA%20FINAL%20slides%2011-15-05.pdf.

Wilson, B.A., Evans, J.J., Alderman, N., Burgess, P.W., & Emslie, H. (1997). Behavioural assessment of the dysexecutive syndrome. In P. Rabbitt (Ed.), **Methodology of Frontal and Executive Function** (pp. 232-241). London: Psychology Press.

Wolf, M.M. (1978). Social validity: The case for subjective measurement or how applied behavior analysis is finding its heart. **Journal of Applied Behavioral Analysis, 11** (2), 203-214.

Zins, J.E., Weissberg, R.P., Wang, M.C., & Walberg, H.J. (Eds.). (2004). **Building academic success on social and emotional learning: What does the research say?** New York: Teachers College Press.

Bibliography

Antshel, K.M., & Remer, R. (2003). Social skills training in children with attention deficit hyperactivity disorder: A randomized-controlled clinical trial. **Journal of Clinical Child and Adolescent Psychology, 32** (1), 153-165.

Arbuthnot, J., & Gordon, D.A. (1986). Behavioral and cognitive effects of a moral reasoning development intervention for high-risk behavior-disordered adolescents. **Journal of Consulting and Clinical Psychology, 54** (2), 208-216.

Blake, C., Wang, W., Cartledge, G., & Gardner, R. (2000). Middle-school students with serious emotional disturbances serve as social skills trainers and reinforcers for peers with SED. **Behavioral Disorders, 25** (4), 280-298.

Cartledge, G., Adedapo, V., & Johnson, C.T. (1998). Teacher and parent assessments of the social competence of inner-city children: Issues of gender within race. **Journal of Negro Education, 67** (2), 115-126.

Cartledge, G., & Loe, S.A. (2001). Cultural diversity and social skill instruction. **Exceptionality: A Special Education Journal, 9** (1-2), 33-46.

Cartledge, G., & Milburn, J.F. (Eds.) (1980). **Teaching social skills to children.** New York: Pergamon Press.

Doughty, J.E. (1997, June). **The effect of a social skills curriculum on student performance.** ERIC Document Reproduction Service (EDRS), ED412260. Paper presented at the Annual Research Colloquium (3rd), Carrollton, GA.

Feng, H., & Cartledge, G. (1996). Social skill assessment of inner city Asian, African, and European American students. **School Psychology Review, 25** (2), 228-239.

Gibbs, J.C., Potter, G.B., Goldstein, A.P., & Brendtro, L.K. (1996). From harassment to helping with antisocial youth: The EQUIP program. **Reclaiming Children and Youth: Journal of Emotional and Behavioral Problems, 5** (1), 40-46.

Goldstein, A.P., & McGinnis, E. (1997). **Skillstreaming the adolescent: New strategies and perspectives for teaching prosocial skills.** Champaign, IL: Research Press.

Greco, L.A., & Morris, T.L. (2001). Treating childhood shyness and related behavior: Empirically evaluated approaches to promote positive social interactions. **Clinical Child and Family Psychology Review, 4** (4), 299-318.

Gresham, F.M. (1997). Social competence and students with behavior disorders: Where we've been, where we are, and where we should go. **Education and Treatment of Children, 20** (3), 233-249.

Gresham, F.M., Noell, G.H., & Elliott, S.N. (1996). Teachers as judges of social competence: A conditional probability analysis. **School Psychology Review, 25** (1), 108-117.

Hansen, D.J., Nangle, D.W., & Meyer, K.A. (1998). Enhancing the effectiveness of social skills interventions with adolescents. **Education and Treatment of Children, 21** (4), 489-513.

Hensley, M., Dillon, J.C., Pratt, D., Ford, J., & Burke, R. (2005). **Tools for teaching social skills in school: Lesson plans, activities, and blended teaching techniques to help your students succeed.** Boys Town, NE: Boys Town Press.

Losel, F., & Beelmann, A. (2003). Effects of child skills training in preventing antisocial behavior: A systematic review of randomized evaluations. **The ANNALS of the American Academy of Political and Social Science, 587** (1), 84-109.

Mellard, D.F., & Hazel, J.S. (1992). Social competencies as a pathway to successful life transitions. **Learning Disability Quarterly, 15** (4), 251-271.

Rivera, B.D., & Atkinson, D.R. (1997). Culturally sensitive interventions: Social skills training with children and parents from culturally and linguistically diverse backgrounds. **Intervention in School and Clinic, 33** (2), 75-80.

Schumaker, J.B. (1992). Social performance of individuals with learning disabilities: Through the looking glass of KU-IRLD research. **School Psychology Review, 21** (3), 387-399.

Spence, S.H., Donovan, C., & Brechman-Toussaint, M. (2000). The treatment of childhood social phobia: The effectiveness of a social skills training-based, cognitive-behavioral intervention, with and without parental involvement. **Journal of Child Psychology and Psychiatry, 41** (6), 713-726.

Taylor, G. (1993). **The relationship between social skills development, academic achievement and interpersonal relations of African-American males.** ERIC Document Reproduction Service (EDRS), ED390819.

Volz, J.R., Snyder, T., & Sterba, M. (2009). **Teaching social skills to youth with mental health disorders.** Boys Town, NE: Boys Town Press.

Webster-Stratton, C., Reid, J., & Hammond, M. (2001). Social skills and problem-solving training for children with early-onset conduct problems: Who benefits? **Journal of Child Psychology and Psychiatry and Allied Disciplines, 42** (7), 941-952.

Zimmerman, D.P. (2002). Research and practice in social- and life-skills training. **Residential Treatment for Children & Youth, 20** (2), 51-75.

Index

F

family
    engagement, 7
    foster, 4, 9, 11, 19, 29
    meetings, 59
    reunification, 4
    -Teachers, 4
fear, 18, 72, 195, 196, 277
feedback, 2, 25, 27, 29, 33-36, 38-39, 41-42, 46, 50, 55, 57-59, 70, 76, 85-86, 114, 178, 183, 190, 199, 224, 225, 268
flexibility, 14, 52
Following Instructions, 2, 7, 22-23, 25, 31, 33-36, 39-40, 45-47, 50, 62, 66, 70, 75, 77-78, 192
Following Rules, 25, 27, 116
Following Safety Rules, 72, 207
Following Through on Agreements and Contracts, 72, 208
Following Written Instructions, 70, 117
Formulating Strategies, 73, 262

G

Gaining Consent, 72, 103, 131, 209-210
gangs, 61, 173
Gathering Information, 73, 263
generalization, 29, 45, 50, 52, 67
    assignment, 53, 56
    definition of, 34, 45
    promoting, 27, 42-43, 46-48
    social skills, 45-48, 56
    train-and-hope approach to, 45
    training, 46
Getting Along with Others, 33
Getting Another Person's Attention, 70, 118
Getting the Teacher's Attention, 25, 46, 70, 119
Giving Compliments, 71, 120
Giving Consent, 72, 211-212
Giving Instructions, 72, 213
Giving Rationales, 72, 214
Greeting Others, 71, 121

Greenspan, Stephen, 2
group teaching, 49-59
    activities for, 53
    advantages of, 49-51
    components, 53
    format and examples of, 49, 53-57
    maintaining a productive atmosphere, 57-58
    presentation of material for, 53
    structure and format, 51-53

H

Harvard University, 14
help
    accepting, 71, 160
    asking for, 70, 102
    offering, 71, 135
hope, 7, 13, 38, 205
hopelessness, 12
humor, 231, 240, 267
hyperactivity, 5, 18, 47

I

Identifying Your Own Feelings, 73, 264
Ignoring Distractions, 40-41, 71, 122
impulse control, 14
incarceration, 2, 19
independent-living skills, 15
Initiating a Conversation, 71, 123
Interrupting Appropriately, 25, 71, 124
Interrupting or Changing Negative or Harmful Thoughts, 73, 265
Interviewing for a Job, 73, 266
Introducing Yourself, 70, 75, 83-84
Introducing Others, 71, 125

J

juvenile delinquency, 2, 19

K

Keeping Property in Its Place, 25, 72, 215

social competence, 7, 15, 17-19, 61

social cues, 13, 26, 28, 47, 71, 72, 162, 228

social skills, 14-15

    academic, 15

    acquisition deficits, 17

    benefits of, 19

    components, 23-26

    curriculum, 69-287

    deficits, 14, 17-21, 24, 33, 36, 64, 67

    ethical/moral, 15

    fluency deficits, 17-18

    generalizing, 45-48

    identifying, 28-29

    independent-living skills, 15

    introducing new, 34

    opportunities for teaching, 29

    performance deficits, 17-18

    reinforcing, 29

    replacement, 25

    role-playing, 38, 43, 45, 53, 55-57, 66

    social competence and, 17-18

    task analysis of, 24-26

    teaching in a group setting, 49-59

    teaching, individual techniques, 27-43

    training, overview of, 17-20

social withdrawal, 18

Staying on Task, 7, 56, 71, 148

Sticking Up for Others, 71, 149

Sticking Up for Yourself, 71, 150

stress, 13, 15, 49, 62, 64, 72, 73, 180, 225, 234, 242, 259, 271

Suggesting an Activity, 72, 239

suicide ideation, 6, 12

T

Taking Risks Appropriately, 73, 282

Talking With Others, 70, 75, 81-82

tantrums, 10, 22

task

    analyzing, 11, 21, 24, 28

    completing, 15, 70, 110, 111, 272

    focusing on, 4

    initiation, 14

    organizing, 14

    prioritizing, 14

    staying on, 24, 56, 71, 148

teasing, 72, 76, 89, 122, 232

time management, 220

Tools for Teaching Social Skills in School, 70

truancy, 63

truthfulness, 107, 139, 181, 189

U

Using an Appropriate Voice Tone (or Level), 71, 152

Using Anger Control (Self-Control) Strategies, 25, 71, 153

Using Appropriate Humor, 71, 240

Using Appropriate Language, 25, 71, 241

Using Community Resources, 73, 284

Using Leisure Time, 73, 285

Using Relaxation Strategies, 25, 72, 242

Using Self-Monitoring and Self-Reflection, 25, 73, 286

Using Self-Talk or Self-Instruction, 73, 243

Using Spontaneous Problem-Solving, 62, 73, 244

Using Strategies to Find a Job, 73, 287

Using Structured Problem-Solving (SODAS), 25, 71, 154

Using Study Skills, 73, 245

Using Table Etiquette, 71, 155

Using Technology Appropriately, 73, 246

V

Valuing Differences, 73, 283

Volunteering, 57, 71, 156

W

Waiting Your Turn, 25, 71, 157

Working Independently, 73, 247

Working with Others, 71, 158

More Social Skill Lesson Plans for the Classroom

Teaching children social skills gives them more behavioral choices – choices that are healthier for them, for you, and for your classroom. When students learn the skills in this lesson plan book, they help create a productive, collaborative, and cooperative learning environment.

In this book, 35 lesson plans with activities will help you introduce to your students a range of social skills, from the basic (following instructions and listening to others) to the complex (advocating for yourself and setting long-term goals).

Lessons are written in an easy-to-follow format with talking points to help you define and explain a skill and guide students through an activity. At the end of each lesson is a *Think Sheet* for students with questions about how to use a skill in different settings and situations. Role-play scenarios are provided so students can practice each skill's behavioral steps. Additional classroom activities blend the teaching of social skills into academic lessons in math/science, language arts, social science, and physical education.

An ideal companion to *Tools for Teaching Social Skills in School*, this workbook features downloadable worksheets and skill posters (to print and hang in classrooms and common areas)! Some of the social skills included are: expressing empathy, going to an assembly, accepting defeat or loss, using anger control (self-control) strategies, responding to inappropriate talk/touch, completing homework, being prepared for class, and resisting negative peer pressure.

More Tools for Teaching Social Skills in School
Midge Odermann Mougey, Ed.D., et al.
ISBN: 978-1-934490-04-4

Available from bookstores or from the Boys Town Press
1-800-282-6657 • BoysTownPress.org

Book Offers Social Skill Lesson Plans for Teachers

Dealing with disruptive behaviors in the classroom can reduce the time a teacher has available for academic teaching. You can help prevent problem behaviors by teaching social skills to students. When children practice and learn how to behave in the classroom, they contribute to creating an environment that's calm, quiet, and conducive to successful learning.

This book provides teachers with:

- Lesson plans for teaching 28 different social skills with activities that can be adapted for students in grades K-12. The plans include suggestions for discussion, activities, journaling, role-play, and reading.

- Reproducible skill pages that you can hand out or post in the classroom as reminders to students, and coupons you can use to reward good behavior.

- Techniques and examples for "blending" the teaching of social skills into academic lessons in reading, writing, math, and social studies.

- Ideas for using bulletin board displays to motivate and monitor behavior.

- Strategies for increasing parent support.

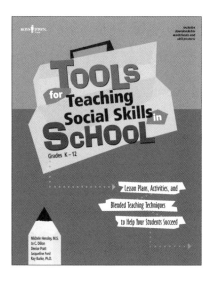

*Tools for Teaching
Social Skills in School*
ISBN: 978-1-889322-64-3

The authors have a combined 40 years of teaching experience in K-12 classrooms, and train teachers, administrators, and other school staff across the United States in the Boys Town Education Model®. The Model emphasizes building relationships with students, teaching social skills, and reinforcement of positive behavior.

Available from bookstores or from the Boys Town Press
1-800-282-6657 • boystownpress.org

The Boys Town Press offers many books and other resources useful to teachers, counselors, other youth-serving professionals, and parents.

For a free catalog, call **1-800-282-6657** or visit **BoysTownPress.org**

Boys Town Press titles by Julia Cook

Kid-friendly books to teach social skills

Reinforce the social skills RJ learns in each book by ordering its corresponding teacher's activity guide and skill posters.

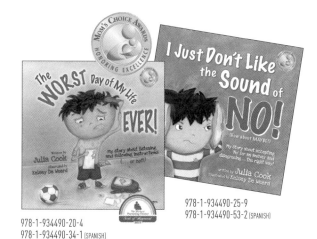

978-1-934490-20-4
978-1-934490-34-1 (SPANISH)

978-1-934490-25-9
978-1-934490-53-2 (SPANISH)

978-1-934490-28-0

978-1-934490-35-8

978-1-934490-43-3

978-1-934490-49-5

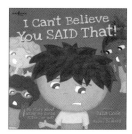

978-1-934490-67-9

A book series to help kids get along.

Building RELATIONSHIPS

978-1-944882-56-3   978-1-944882-24-2

OTHER TITLES: Cliques Just Don't Make Cents; Tease Monster; Table Talk; Peer Pressure Gauge; Hygiene...You Stink!; I Want to Be the Only Dog; The Judgmental Flower

A book series to help kids master the art of communicating.

COMMUNICATE with Confidence

978-1-944882-13-6   979-8-88907-000-9

OTHER TITLES: Gas Happens; Well, I Can Top That!

Help kids take responsibility for their behavior.

Responsible ME!

978-1-934490-90-7   978-1-934490-98-3

OTHER TITLES: The Procrastinator; But It's Not My Fault; Cheaters Never Prosper

---

Help kids overcome their fears, learn essential social skills, and have healthier, happier relationships.

978-1-944882-51-8

978-1-944882-58-7

Socially Skilled Kids

OTHER TITLES: Herman Jiggle, It's Recess,

Other Books by Julia Cook

978-1-944882-19-8

978-1-944882-37-2

BOYS TOWN Press®

BoysTownPress.org

For information on Boys Town, its Education Model®, Common Sense Parenting®, and training programs:
LiftwithBoysTown.org | boystown.org/parenting
training@BoysTown.org | 1-800-545-5771

For parenting and educational books and other resources:
BoysTownPress.org
btpress@BoysTown.org | 1-800-282-6657

Executive FUNction

Stories that teach children how to plan, organize, manage time, and maintain self-control!

Reviewed by Licensed Mental Health Therapists for Recognition of Quality in the Field

Boys Town Press books by Bryan Smith

978-1-944882-72-3

978-1-944882-45-7

978-1-944882-60-0

978-1-934490-96-9

978-1-944882-31-0

978-1-944882-20-4

978-1-944882-11-2

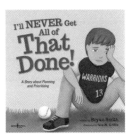

978-1-944882-50-1

OTHER TITLES: My Day Is Ruined!; What's the Problem?

Young readers learn how to be more giving, more understanding, and more resilient!

978-1-944882-36-5

978-1-944882-29-7

978-1-944882-12-9

978-1-944882-46-4

OTHER TITLES: Kindness Counts; Everyone's Contributions Count; Speak Up for Yourself

By author Jennifer Law

978-1-944882-49-5

978-1-944882-70-9

By author Kimberly Delude

978-1-944882-25-9

978-1-944882-17-4

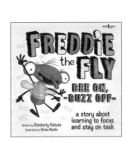

978-1-944882-34-1

Call 1-800-282-6657 or visit BoysTownPress.org

Chapter Books That Teach

Grades 4-8
by author Leona Lugan

The Middle School Misfits series is great for independent readers and middle school students will relate to the challenges and joys that Jilly and her schoolmates experience in this timeless tale about facing your fears and making new friends.

978-1-944882-35-8

By author Melissa Minery

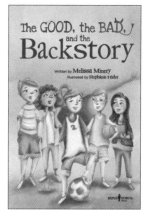

978-1-944882-71-6

Grades 3-7 by author Tony Penn

The Michael McMichaels series is a collection of funny, fast-paced stories that will turn the most reluctant readers into reading machines. The cast of characters includes Michael, a mischievous third-grader, his loyal friend Kenny and their always-annoying classmate Harriet.

978-1-944882-32-7

978-1-944882-21-1

978-1-944882-10-5

TITLES INCLUDE: The Case of the Escaping Elephants; The Double-Dog Dare!; The Creepy Campers; The Borrowed Bracelet; The Angry Alligator

Comic Books for Grades 3-8 by author Kip Jones

URBAN CHARACTER EDUCATION

Rhymes, rap lyrics, mnemonic devices, and graphic illustrations made this series a Mom's Choice Awards Gold winner!

978-1-934490-66-2

978-1-934490-79-2

978-1-934490-92-1

978-1-944882-06-8

Jennifer Licate
GRADES 4-8

A book series and accompanying activity guides focused on changing friendships, finding your place, advocating for yourself, and being true to who you are.

978-1-944882-63-1

978-1-944882-65-5

978-1-944882-67-9

978-1-944882-89-1

Press

Call 1-800-282-6657 or visit **BoysTownPress.org**